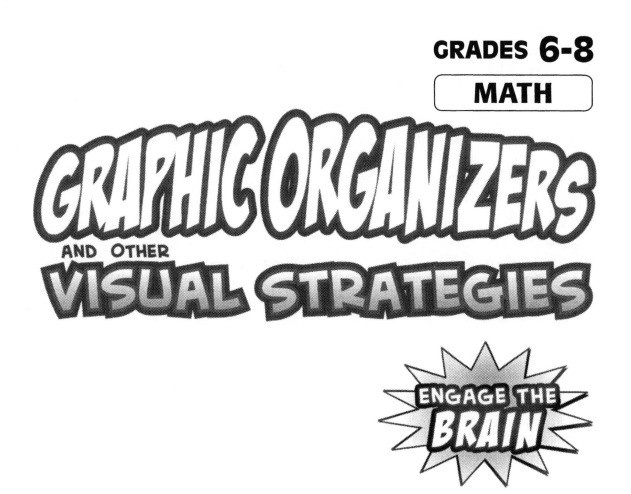

GRAPHIC ORGANIZERS
AND OTHER
VISUAL STRATEGIES

ENGAGE THE
BRAIN

MARCIA L. TATE

CORWIN PRESS
Classroom

For information:

Corwin Press
A SAGE Publications Company
2455 Teller Road
Thousand Oaks, California 91320
CorwinPress.com

SAGE Publications, Ltd.
1 Oliver's Yard
55 City Road
London EC1Y 1SP
United Kingdom

SAGE Publications India Pvt. Ltd.
B 1/I 1 Mohan Cooperative
Industrial Area
Mathura Road, New Delhi
India 110 044

SAGE Publications Asia-Pacific Pvt. Ltd.
33 Pekin Street #02-01
Far East Square
Singapore 048763

ISBN 978-1-4129-5231-6

This book is printed on acid-free paper.

08 09 10 11 12 10 9 8 7 6 5 4 3 2 1

Executive Editor: Kathleen Hex
Managing Developmental Editor: Christine Hood
Editorial Assistant: Anne O'Dell
Developmental Writers: Susan Ludwig and Carrie Ryan
Developmental Editor: Karen P. Hall
Proofreader: Bette Darwin
Art Director: Anthony D. Paular
Cover Designer: Monique Hahn
Interior Production Artist: Scott Van Atta
Illustrator: Derrick Chow
Design Consultant: PUMPKiN PIE Design

GRADES **6-8**
MATH

ENGAGE THE BRAIN

TABLE OF CONTENTS

Connections to Standards

This chart shows the national mathematics standards that are covered in each chapter.

NUMBERS AND OPERATIONS	Standards are covered on pages
Understand numbers, ways of representing numbers, relationships among numbers, and number systems.	9, 14, 17, 20, 24
Understand meanings of operations and how they relate to one another.	14, 20, 24, 41
Compute fluently and make reasonable estimates.	31, 52, 71, 87, 91

ALGEBRA	Standards are covered on pages
Understand patterns, relations, and functions.	28, 31, 34, 37, 41, 56
Represent and analyze mathematical situations and structures using algebraic symbols.	20, 28, 34, 37, 41, 52, 56, 61
Use mathematical models to represent and understand quantitative relationships.	9, 17, 24, 34, 37, 41, 68, 71, 74
Analyze change in various contexts.	28, 31, 34, 41, 56

GEOMETRY	Standards are covered on pages
Analyze characteristics and properties of two- and three-dimensional geometric shapes, and develop mathematical arguments about geometric relationships.	44, 47, 52, 61, 74
Specify locations and describe spatial relationships using coordinate geometry and other representational systems.	56
Apply transformations and use symmetry to analyze mathematical situations.	47, 56
Use visualization, spatial reasoning, and geometric modeling to solve problems.	24, 44, 47, 52, 56, 61, 71, 74

MEASUREMENT	Standards are covered on pages
Understand measurable attribute of objects and the units, systems, and processes of measurement.	44, 52, 64, 68, 71, 74, 91
Apply appropriate techniques, tools, and formulas to determine measurements.	44, 52, 61, 64, 68, 71, 74, 91

DATA ANALYSIS AND PROBABILITY	Standards are covered on pages
Formulate questions that can be addressed with data, and collect, organize, and display relevant data to answer them.	31, 79, 82, 87, 91
Select and use appropriate statistical methods to analyze data.	79, 82, 87
Develop and evaluate inferences and predictions that are based on data.	79, 82, 87, 91
Understand and apply basic concepts of probability.	87, 91

PROBLEM SOLVING	Standards are covered on pages
Build new mathematical knowledge through problem solving.	9, 17, 28, 31, 34, 52, 61, 82, 87, 91
Solve problems that arise in mathematics and in other contexts.	9, 17, 28, 31, 34, 52, 61, 82, 87, 91
Apply and adapt a variety of appropriate strategies to solve problems.	9, 17, 28, 31, 34, 52, 61, 82, 87, 91
Monitor and reflect on the process of mathematical problem solving.	9, 17, 28, 31, 34, 52, 61, 82, 87, 91

REASONING AND PROOF	Standards are covered on pages
Recognize reasoning and proof as fundamental aspects of mathematics.	31, 44, 52
Make and investigate mathematical conjectures.	14, 31, 44, 52, 91
Develop and evaluate mathematical arguments and proofs.	44, 52
Select and use various types of reasoning and methods of proof.	44, 52

COMMUNICATION	Standards are covered on pages
Organize and consolidate mathematical thinking through communication.	9, 14, 31, 34, 37, 44, 47, 61, 64, 68, 79, 87, 91
Communicate mathematical thinking coherently and clearly to peers, teachers, and others.	9, 14, 31, 34, 37, 44, 47, 61, 64, 68, 79, 87, 91
Analyze and evaluate the mathematical thinking and strategies of others.	9, 14, 31, 34, 37, 44, 47, 61, 64, 68, 79, 87, 91
Use the language of mathematics to express mathematical ideas precisely.	9, 14, 31, 34, 37, 44, 47, 61, 64, 68, 79, 87, 91

Introduction

An ancient Chinese proverb claims: "Tell me, I forget. Show me, I remember. Involve me, I understand." This timeless saying insinuates what all educators should know: Unless students are involved and actively engaged in learning, true learning rarely occurs.

The latest brain research reveals that both the right and left hemispheres of the brain should be engaged in the learning process. This is important because the hemispheres talk to one another over the corpus callosum, the structure that connects them. No strategies are better designed for this purpose than graphic organizers and visuals. Both of these strategies engage students' visual modality. More information goes into the brain visually than through any other modality. Therefore, it makes sense to take advantage of students' visual strengths to reinforce and make sense of learning.

How to Use This Book

Correlated with the national standards for math, the activities in this book cover the content areas and are designed using strategies that actively engage the brain. They are presented in the way the brain learns best, to make sure students get the most out of each lesson: focus activity, modeling guided practice, check for understanding, independent practice, and closing. Go through each step to ensure that students will be fully engaged in the concept being taught and understand its purpose and meaning.

Each step-by-step activity provides one or more visual tools students can use to make important connections between related concepts, structure their thinking, organize ideas logically, and reinforce learning. Graphic organizers and visuals include: Venn diagram, number web, relationship map, data table, coordinate map, circle graph, probability map, stem-and-leaf plot, box-and-whisker plot, word web, picture model, compare-and-contrast map, 3-D models, and more!

These brain-compatible activities are sure to engage and motivate every student's brain in your classroom! Watch your students change from passive to active learners as they process visual concepts into learning that is not only fun, but also remembered for a lifetime.

Put It Into Practice

Lecture and repetitive worksheets have long been the traditional way of delivering knowledge and reinforcing learning. While some higher-achieving students may engage in this type of learning, educators now know that actively engaging students' brains is not a luxury, but a necessity if students are truly to acquire and retain content, not only for tests, but for life.

The 1990s were dubbed the Decade of the Brain, because millions of dollars were spent on brain research. Educators today should know more about how students learn than ever before. Learning style theories that call for student engagement have been proposed for decades, as evidenced by research such as Howard Gardner's theory of multiple intelligences (1983), Bernice McCarthy's 4MAT Model (1990), and VAKT (visual, auditory, kinesthetic, tactile) learning styles theories.

I have identified 20 strategies that, according to brain research and learning style theory, appear to correlate with the way the brain learns best. I have observed hundreds of teachers—regular education, special education, and gifted. Regardless of the classification or grade level of the students, exemplary teachers consistently use these 20 strategies to deliver memorable classroom instruction and help their students understand and retain vast amounts of content.

These 20 brain-based instructional strategies include the following:

1. Brainstorming and Discussion

2. Drawing and Artwork

3. Field Trips

4. Games

5. Graphic Organizers, Semantic Maps, and Word Webs

6. Humor

7. Manipulatives, Experiments, Labs, and Models

8. Metaphors, Analogies, and Similes

9. Mnemonic Devices

10. Movement

11. Music, Rhythm, Rhyme, and Rap

12. Project-based and Problem-based Instruction

13. Reciprocal Teaching and Cooperative Learning

14. Role Plays, Drama, Pantomimes, Charades

15. Storytelling

16. Technology

17. Visualization and Guided Imagery

18. Visuals

19. Work Study and Apprenticeships

20. Writing and Journals

This book features Strategy 5: Graphic Organizers, Semantic Maps, and Word Webs, and Strategy 18: Visuals. Both of these strategies focus on integrating the visual and verbal elements of learning. Picture thinking, visual thinking, and visual/spatial learning is the phenomenon of thinking through visual processing. Since 90% of the brain's sensory input comes from visual sources, it stands to reason that the most powerful influence on learners' behavior is concrete, visual images. (Jensen, 1994) In addition, linking verbal and visual images increases students' ability to store and retrieve information. (Ogle, 2000)

Graphic organizers are visual representations of linear ideas that benefit both left and right hemispheres of the brain. They assist us in making sense of information, enable us to search for patterns, and provide an organized tool for making important conceptual connections. Graphic organizers, also known as word webs or semantic, mind, and concept maps, can be used to plan lessons or present information to students. Once familiar with the technique, students should be able to construct their own graphic organizers, reflecting their understanding of the concepts taught.

Because we live in a highly visual world, using visuals as a teaching strategy makes sense. Each day, students are overwhelmed with images from video games, computers, and television. Visual strategies capitalize specifically on the one modality that many students use consistently and have developed extensively—the visual modality. Types of visuals include overheads, maps, graphs, charts, and other concrete objects and artifacts that clarify learning. Since so much sensory input comes from visual sources, pictures, words, and learning-related artifacts around the classroom take on exaggerated importance in students' brains. Visuals such as these provide learning support and constant reinforcement.

These memorable strategies help students make sense of learning by focusing on the ways the brain learns best. Fully supported by the latest brain research, these strategies provide the tools you need to boost motivation, energy, and most important, the academic achievement of your students.

CHAPTER 1

Numbers and Operations

Running Project: Visual Model

Skills Objectives

Identify and compare fractions, decimals, and percents.
Use mathematical models to represent and understand quantitative relationships.
Apply and explain different strategies to solve problems.

Materials
Fraction Strips reproducible

Running Project Data reproducible

Running Project Analysis reproducible

rulers

colored pencils

scissors

resealable plastic bags

A **Visual Model** can help students more thoroughly understand abstract concepts and move beyond simple memorization and numerical computation. By creating and using visual models to see and compare math concepts, students are better able to understand and apply their math skills. In this activity, students create and use fraction models to help them visualize and conceptualize parts of a whole.

1. Invite students to share what they know about fractions. Ask: *What is a fraction? What is a numerator? What is a denominator? Where do you see fractions?*

2. Write the following patterns on the board for students to analyze and compare. Draw large circles or rectangles on the board and divide them by halves to help illustrate each pattern. Point out that all three patterns decrease by the same amount (dividing by 1/2): *1/2 (half), 1/4 (fourth), 1/8 (eighth); 1/3 (third), 1/6 (sixth), 1/12 (twelfth); 1/5 (fifth), 1/10 (tenth).*

3. Draw a long number line from 0 to 1 on the board, and label the 1/2 mark. Invite volunteers to write each pattern of fractions on the number line. Point out that all of the fractions are *unit fractions* less than 1/2. Then ask students to name and write greater fractions on the number line. For example: *What is a fraction between 1/2 and 1? What is a fraction between 5/6 and 1? What is a fraction between 1/3 and 2/3 that has a denominator of 8?* (Possible answers: *2/3, 9/10, 5/8*) Invite students to explain how they came up with each answer.

4. Then give each student a ruler and a copy of the **Fraction Strips reproducible (page 11)**, and use a copy to guide instruction. Demonstrate how to measure and divide each fraction strip into

equal parts as indicated. Tell students to write the unit fraction on each section and lightly color each set using a different color. Check students' work before they cut apart their fraction strips into separate sections. Have them store their cut-up fraction strips in a resealable plastic bag.

5. Give students a copy of the **Running Project Data** and **Running Project Analysis reproducibles (pages 12–13)**. Review all the directions with students, and do the first row of the table together. Check that students understand how to complete the rest of the pages before having them finish on their own or with a partner.

6. Monitor students as they work, offering assistance as needed. Check that students are completing the data table and bar graph correctly. Remind them to write all fractions in simplest form. Point out that the bar graph should show how much each runner has completed of his or her own goal (percent or fraction of the whole). Encourage students to use their fraction strips to help them complete each bar.

7. Review and discuss the answers together. Invite volunteers to read aloud their answers, and have the rest of the class give a thumbs-up if they agree. If they don't agree, have those students share their answers, and ask the entire class to determine who is correct. Make sure students understand and can recognize multiple representations of the same amount, such as 1/2, 0.50, 50%.

Extended Learning

- Have students complete their own running project, setting a mileage goal and time frame, and then use a data table and bar graph to show their progress.

- Ask students to write about possible variables that could affect each student's running progress and suggest ways to reduce or eliminate those variables.

Fraction Strips

Directions: Use a ruler to measure and divide each fraction strip into the fractional parts shown.

Halves

Fourths

Eighths

Thirds

Sixths

Twelfths

Fifths

Tenths

Running Project Data

Directions: Complete the table and bar graph about the Running Project. Shade the bars to show each student's progress after six days. Use fraction strips to help you.

Students at Franklin Middle School are participating in the Running Project. Each student chose a goal for the number of miles to run over a ten-day period. After six days:

- Keisha has completed 84 laps, and her goal is to run 30 miles.
- Adam has completed 50% of his goal of running 40 miles.
- Bob has completed 2/5 of his 25-mile goal.
- Each lap is 1/4 of a mile.

	Goal Miles/Laps	Laps Completed	Fraction	Decimal	Percent
Keisha		84			
Adam					50%
Bob			$\frac{40}{100} = \frac{2}{5}$		

Keisha

Adam

Bob

Running Project Analysis

Directions: Use the Running Project Data sheet to answer these questions.

1. In order to reach his or her goal, how many laps should each student run per day in order to run the same amount every day?

_____

_____

_____

2. After six days, how many total laps should each student have completed? Compare those values to the values in the table. Who is reaching his or her goal so far?

_____

_____

_____

3. On the number line, show each student's progress after six days. Who has the highest fraction of his or her goal completed? Who has the least?

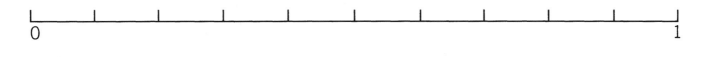

_____

4. How many more laps should each student run in order to reach his or her goal?

_____

_____

5. If the students want to achieve 150% of their goal, how many laps should they run? What is the amount as a fraction? Is the fraction greater than or less than 1?

_____

_____

Follow the Orders: Sequence Chart

Materials

Order of Operations reproducible

math journals

Skills Objectives

Identify, describe, and apply the order of operations to simplify equations.

Use and explain different strategies to solve problems.

A **Sequence Chart** is an excellent visual tool to help students follow a step-by-step process in mathematics, such as following the orders of operations to simplify equations. The graphic organizer also provides a clear visual path for students to recheck and correct their work for accuracy and completion.

1. Write $6^2 \div 4 + 3(8 - 4) \cdot 5 - 2$ on the board, and list the following words to the left of it: *parentheses, exponent, multiplication, division, addition, subtraction*. Invite volunteers to match each name to its correct symbol in the equation and to explain its operation (method of computation). Point out that multiplication can be shown in different ways—using an *x*, a dot, or a number in front of parentheses.

2. Give students a copy of the **Order of Operations reproducible (page 16)**, and draw a copy on the board to guide instruction. Demonstrate how to simplify the equation $6^2 \div 4 + 3 (8 - 4) \cdot 5 - 2$ step by step, following the order of operations. (You might have students copy the following summary in their math journals.)

Order of Operations

P–First solve inside the underline{p}arentheses.

E–Then simplify underline{e}xponents.

M or D–underline{M}ultiply or underline{d}ivide, whichever comes first, from left to right.

A or S–Then underline{a}dd or underline{s}ubtract, whichever comes first, from left to right.

Remember: PEMDAS–underline{P}lease underline{E}xcuse underline{M}y underline{D}ear Aunt underline{S}ally.

3. Write each step of the simplification in the sequence chart as students do the same on their reproducible. Next to each downward arrow, write and circle the first letter of the operation used in the subsequent box. For example, multiplication: (M) ↓.

4. Write the following incomplete equations on the board for students to simplify using more copies of the sequence chart or by drawing their own. Suggest that they use the "guess and check" method to see which operational symbols will work for each given answer. Remind students to follow the order of operations. Explain that they may use two of the 5s as a fraction (5/5) or as an exponent (5^5), and that each equation may have more than one possible solution.

   5 5 5 5 5 = 4
   5 5 5 5 5 = 5
   5 5 5 5 5 = 6
   5 5 5 5 5 = 8
   5 5 5 5 5 = 15

5. Invite students to show their solutions on the board and explain how they solved each equation. Have classmates check the solutions and offer others. For example:

   $(5 + 5 + 5 + 5) \div 5 = 4$
   $(5 - 5) \cdot 5 \cdot 5 + 5 = 5$
   $(5 - 5) + (5 + 5/5) = 6$
   $(5 + 5 + 5) \div 5 + 5 = 8$
   $(5 + 5 + 5) + (5 - 5) = 15$

Extended Learning

Invite students to write and simplify more challenging equations that include algebraic expressions, variables, and bracketed terms. Explain that terms within brackets are solved first before solving inside parentheses.

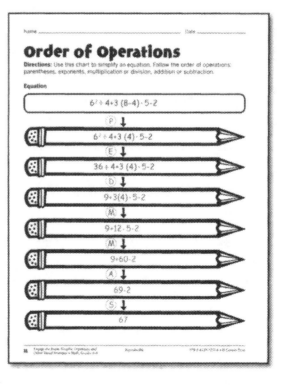

Name _____ Date _____

Order of Operations

Directions: Use this chart to simplify an equation. Follow the order of operations: parentheses, exponents, multiplication or division, addition or subtraction.

Equation

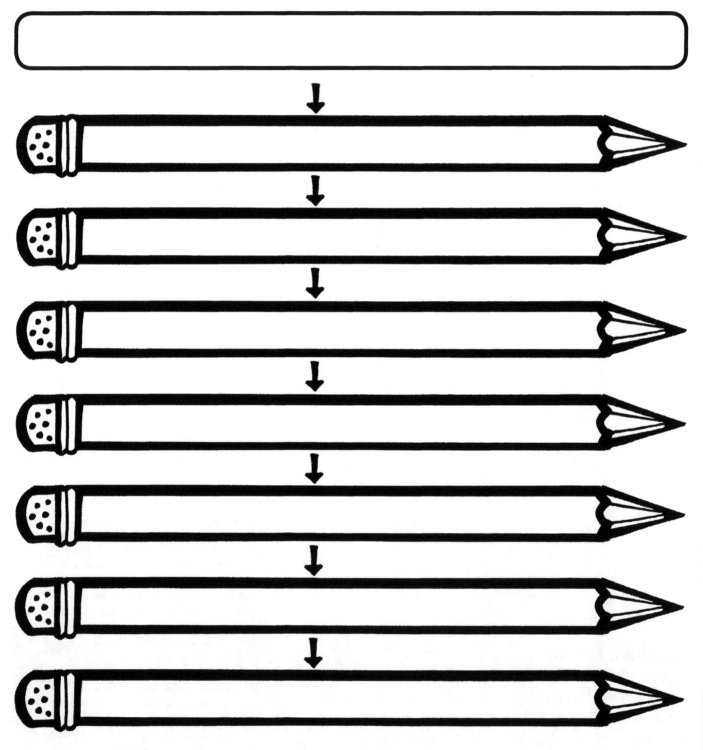

Engage the Brain: Graphic Organizers and Other Visual Strategies • Math, Grades 6–8   Reproducible   978-1-4129-5231-6 • © Corwin Press

Common Factors: Venn Diagram

Skills Objectives
Find the greatest common factor (GCF) using prime factorization and a Venn diagram.

Apply different strategies and use mathematical models to solve problems.

Materials
Venn Diagrams reproducible

A **Venn Diagram** is a graphic organizer that helps students compare and contrast information. For math, it can be used to solve problems involving relationships between intersecting sets of data. In this activity, students use a Venn diagram to find the greatest common factor and to solve comparative word problems. The common values are placed in the overlapping section of the diagram.

1. Write *40* and *60* on the board, and review with students how to find the prime factorization of each number by using a factor tree. *(40 = 2 • 2 • 2 • 5; 60 = 2 • 2 • 3 • 5)* Remind students that all of the final answers should be prime numbers.

2. Then draw a Venn diagram of two overlapping circles. Explain to students that a Venn diagram can be used to compare sets of values. Label one circle *40* and the other *60*. In the overlapping section of the circles, write the prime factors that *40* and *60* have in common *(2, 2, 5)*. In the outer part of each circle, write the remaining prime factors of that number *(2 for 40; 3 for 60)*.

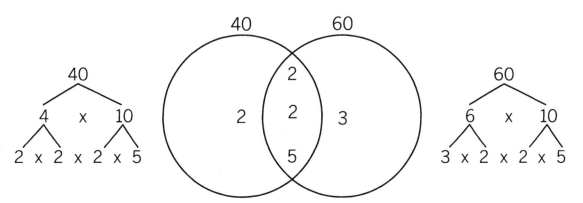

3. Explain to students that the numbers in the center of the diagram can be multiplied together to find the Greatest Common Factor (GCF) of 40 and 60. Invite a volunteer to write that answer below the diagram. *(GCF = 2 • 2 • 5 = 20)*

4. Give students a copy of the **Venn Diagrams reproducible (page 19)**, and have them find the GCF for each of these sets: (1) 36 and 84; (2) 72 and 108; (3) 32, 48, and 56. Point out that the third example is for a triple Venn diagram, which means finding the common factors of all three numbers.

(GCF for 36 and 84 = 12; GCF for 72 and 108 = 36; GCF for 32, 48, and 56 = 8)

5. Invite students to share and compare their results. Confirm the correct answers.

Extended Learning

Have students use another copy of the Venn Diagrams reproducible to solve the following problems. Solve the first problem together and check for understanding before having students complete the rest on their own or with a partner.

- *At Ridley High, 25 students are on the basketball team; 15 students are on the swim team; and 5 are on both the basketball and swim teams. How many students play basketball only? How many total students are there? (25 – 5 = 20 students in basketball only; 20 basketball + 10 swimming + 5 both = 35 in all)*

- *At Ridley High, 58 students play guitar; 47 students play piano; and 20 students play both guitar and piano. How many students play only one instrument? (38 guitar only + 27 piano only = 65 in all play guitar or piano)*

- *A Language Department Survey obtained the following data from 148 students: 78 took Spanish; 56 took Latin; 87 took Portuguese; 26 took Spanish and Latin; 37 took Spanish and Portuguese; 25 took Latin and Portuguese; and 15 took all three languages. How many students took only Spanish? (30) Only Latin? (20) Only Portuguese? (40) Only one language? (90) Only two languages? (43) Latin and Portuguese but not Spanish? (10) Spanish and Latin but not Portuguese? (11)*

(Possible solution: Starting in the center of the Venn diagram, write *15* in the triple overlap section. Subtract the 15 trilingual students from 26, 37, and 25—so those students are not counted more than once—leaving *11*, *22*, and *10* for the double overlap sections. The number of students who took only one language is determined by finding the difference between the total number of students for that language; subtract the bi- and trilingual students that also took that language.)

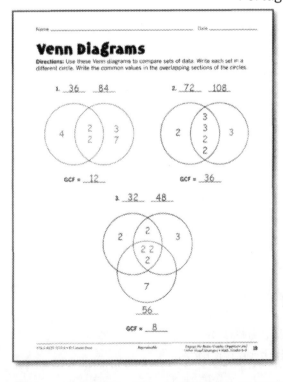

Venn Diagrams

Directions: Use these Venn diagrams to compare sets of data. Write each set in a different circle. Write the common values in the overlapping sections of the circles.

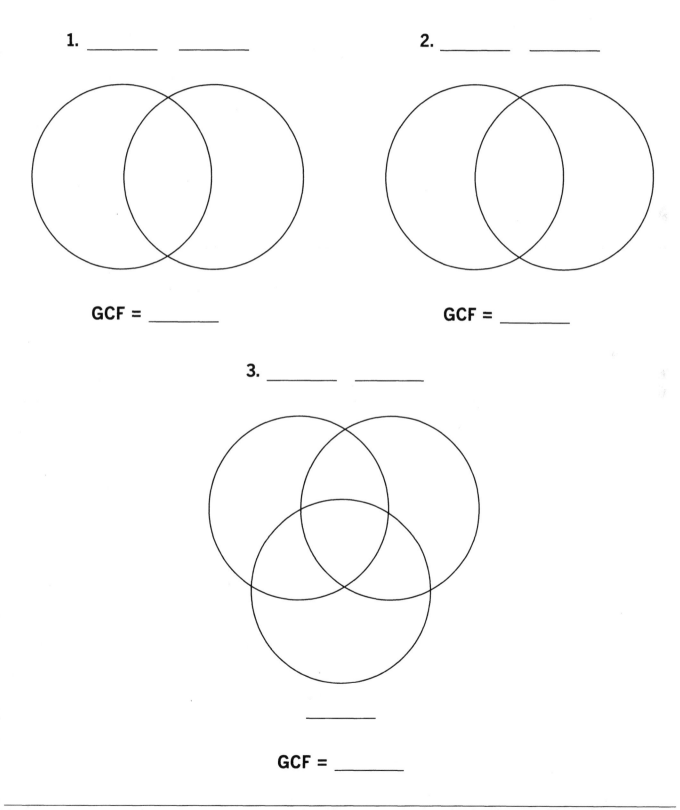

1. _____   _____

GCF = _____

2. _____   _____

GCF = _____

3. _____   _____

_____

GCF = _____

Number Properties: Cluster Chart

Materials

Property Cards reproducible

Number Properties Cluster Chart reproducible

scissors

resealable plastic bags

Skills Objectives

Identify, sort, and compare properties of real numbers (commutative, associative, identity, distributive) using words, numerals, and algebraic expressions.

Using a **Cluster Chart** can help students organize and compare the properties of real numbers for easier recall. By using the graphic organizer to list the properties, rules and definitions, algebraic expressions, and examples, students are able to see a more complete picture of the interrelationship of all the properties.

1. Copy and cut apart the **Property Cards reproducible (page 22)**. Make a set of cards for each small group of students. (Write your own examples in the blank boxes.) Store each set in a separate resealable bag, and save them for the end of the activity.

2. Write *Properties* on the board, and invite students to predict the content of the lesson. Explain that they will be making a chart to help them learn important properties, or rules, about numbers. Give students a copy of the **Number Properties Cluster Chart reproducible (page 23)**, and display a copy to guide instruction.

3. Write *Properties of Real Numbers* in the top box, and ask: *What are the four main properties of real numbers?* Have students write the answers *Commutative, Associative, Identity,* and *Distributive* in the four ovals.

4. Then work together with students to write a rule or description of each property in the first box below each oval. Remind students to include both addition and multiplication. Point out that subtraction and division are *not* commutative.

Commutative Property	Identity Property
The order of the addends or factors does not change the sum or product. $a + b = b + a$ $a \cdot b = b \cdot a$	Any number plus 0 is that number. Any number times 1 is that number. $a + 0 = a \quad a \cdot 1 = a$
Associative Property	**Distributive Property**
The grouping of addends or factors does not change the sum or product. $(a + b) + c = a + (b + c)$ $(a \cdot b) \cdot c = a \cdot (b \cdot c)$	Multiplying a sum by a number is the same as multiplying each addend by that number and then adding the two products. $a \cdot (b + c) = (a \cdot b) + (a \cdot c)$

5. In the second box below each property, have students write one or two number sentences as examples. Invite volunteers to share their examples on the board.

6. For the last set of boxes, work together with students to write a helpful hint or a real-life connection about each property (for easier recall). For example:

   Commutative Property: *Commuters; traveling from A to B is the same as B to A.*

   Associative Property: *Associating with people; rearranging groups of people.*

   Identity Property: *Your identity; it doesn't change when you add 0.*

   Distributive Property: *Distribution; giving paper to students together versus apart.*

7. Divide the class into groups of three or four students, and give each group a bag of property cards to sort into the four properties. Suggest that they refer to their cluster chart. For more fun, have them race to see who finishes first.

8. Review and discuss the results together as a class. Have students take turns reading aloud the cards they put in each category and explaining their decisions.

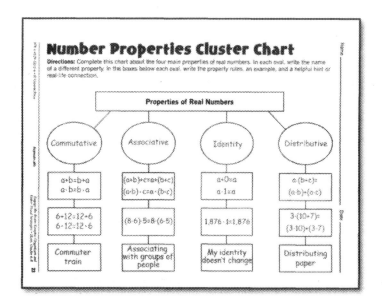

Property Cards

Commutative Property	Associative Property	Identity Property	Distributive Property
$a + b = b + a$	$(a + b) + c = a + (b + c)$	$a \cdot 1 = a$	$a(b + c) = ab + ac$
$2 + 3 = 3 + 2$	$(5 + 6) + 7 = 5 + (6 + 7)$	$a + 0 = a$	$3(9 + 2) = 3(9) + 3(2)$
$45t = t45$	$6(xy) = (6x)y$	$6 \cdot 1 = 6$	$3(3x + 4) = 9x + 12$
$(x + y) + 2 = (y + x) + 2$	$(x + y) + 2 = x + (y + 2)$	$4 + 0 = 4$	$-4(3f - 8) = -12 + 32$
$(1 + 5) + 3 = (5 + 1) + 3$	$(ab)c = a(bc)$	$100 + 0 = 100$	$6a + 6b = 6(a + b)$

Number Properties Cluster Chart

Directions: Complete this chart about the four main properties of real numbers. In each oval, write the name of a different property. In the boxes below each oval, write the property rules, an example, and a helpful hint or real-life connection.

Properties of Real Numbers

Creating Math Problems: Number Webs

Materials

Number Webs
reproducible

More Number Webs
reproducible

calculators (optional)

Skills Objectives

Write and solve a variety of math problems for a specific target number.
Use mathematical models to represent and understand quantitative
relationships.

A **Number Web** is a graphic organizer that can be used to display a
variety of numerical calculations and math concepts. The web consists
of a target number in the center of a geometric web surrounded by
math problems that equal that amount. The
number web provides an opportunity
for students to access their prior
knowledge of math concepts,
make mathematical connections,
and apply their understanding of
new math skills in a creative and
artistic format.

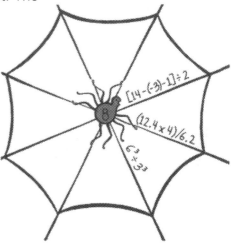

1. Have the class brainstorm
   a list of math topics, and
   write their suggestions on the
   board. For example:

Basic Operations (+, -, x, ÷)	Money
Integers	Time
Fractions	Geometric Shapes
Decimals	Length
Percents	Perimeter
Exponents	Area
Square Roots	Volume
Probability	Surface Area
Mean, Median, Mode	Mass and Weight
Ratios	Scientific Notation
Proportions	Simplifying Expressions
Inequalities	Story Problems

2. Give students a copy of the **Number Webs reproducible (page 26)**, and
   display a copy to guide instruction. Explain to students that, in
   each section of the web, they will write a math problem whose
   answer equals the number in the center. For example, the triangular
   web should have three problems, each with the answer 3.

3. Work together as a class to complete the triangular web. Invite volunteers to write a problem in each section of the triangle. Explain that each problem must involve different math skills and may *not* be a simple calculation such as 7 – 4 = 3. Remind them that all answers must equal 3. For example:

- Division Problem: $1{,}452 \div 484 = 3$

- Order of Operations: $(2^2 + 6)^2 - (9 \cdot 10) - 7 = 3$

- Fractions: $1/2 + 2/3 + 1\,5/6 = 3$

4. Have students complete the rectangular web on their own. Remind them to write four problems that have the answer 4. Encourage students to write multistep problems. Monitor as they work, and offer assistance as needed. You may also provide calculators.

5. Have students exchange papers and check each other's work. Invite volunteers to share their problems on the board for the whole class to solve. Point out any similarities in the problems and strategies used to write and solve each problem.

6. For more practice, have students complete the **More Number Webs reproducible (page 27)** and check each other's work.

Extended Learning

Have students write multistep word problems in each number web, writing a different step or a new problem in each section. For example, the triangular web should have a three-step word problem with the final answer of 3.

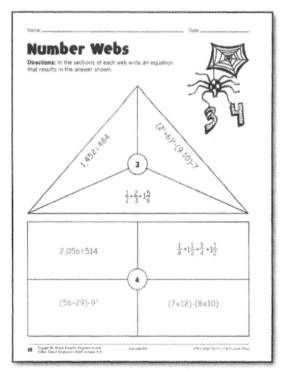

Number Webs

Directions: In the sections of each web, write an equation that results in the answer shown.

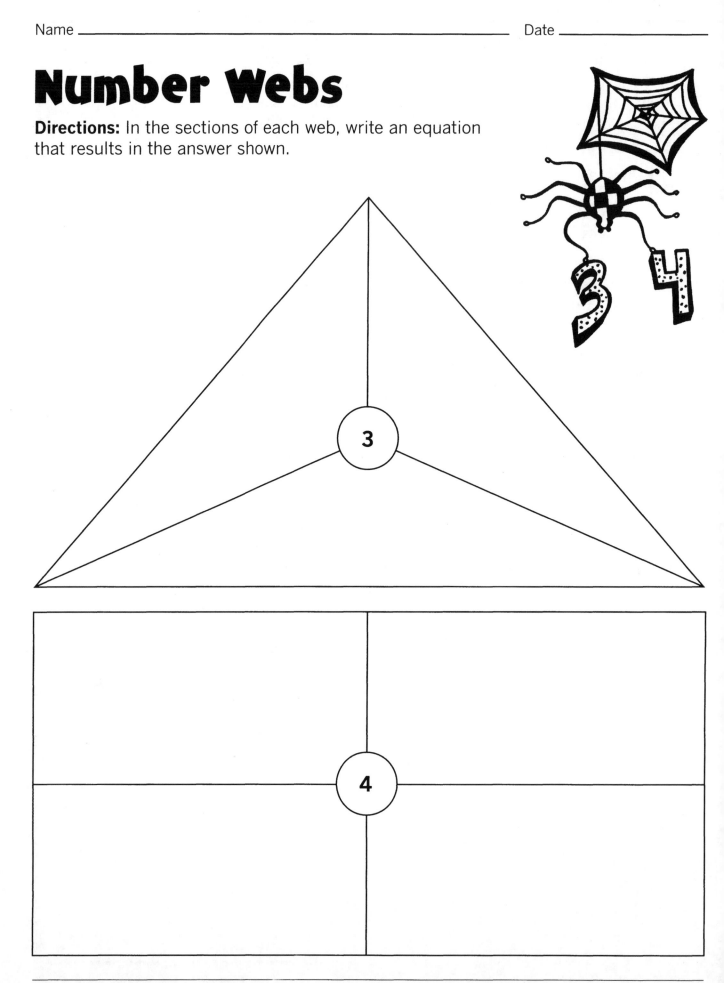

3

4

More Number Webs

Directions: In the sections of each web, write an equation that results in the answer shown.

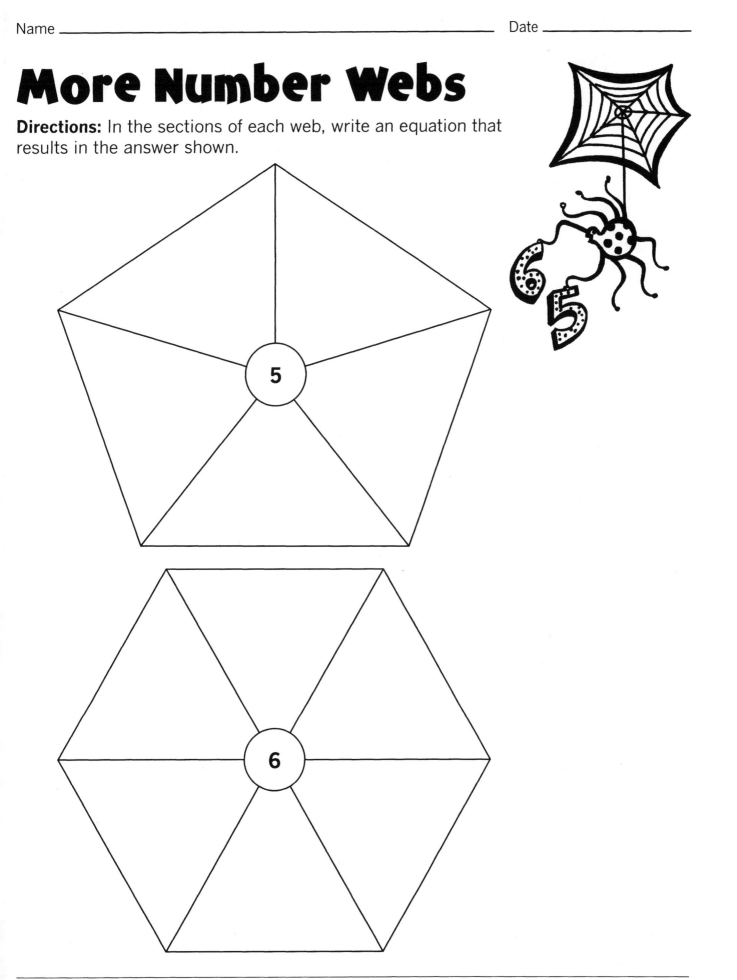

Input–Output Machines: Cause and Effect Map

Materials

Input–Output
Machines
reproducible

Input–Output
Problems
reproducible

Skills Objectives

Interpret and use function notation to identify variables and solve problems.

Use algebraic expressions to represent and analyze mathematical situations.

A **Cause and Effect Map** typically shows the relationship between a cause and its effect. In this activity, students use a modified version to show the relationship between the input and output values in a "function machine." The domain values of x are the input (cause) and the range values of $f(x)$ are the output (effect).

1. Review with students how to read function notation such as $f(x) = 2x^2 - 1$. Point out that $f(x)$ is read as "f of x" or "the function of x" and is used in place of y.

2. Give students two copies of the **Input–Output Machines reproducible (page 29)**, and display a large copy of the machine to guide instruction. Write $f(x) = 2x^2 - 1$ on the machine, and tell students that it is the "directions" or the *function rule* for that machine. Explain that each machine causes the numbers put inside of it to change by a specific function—a cause-and-effect relationship.

3. Demonstrate how the machine works by writing the input (cause) numbers –2, –1, 0, 1, 2 in the top boxes, and writing the output (effect) numbers 7, 1, –1, 1, 7 in the bottom boxes. Work with students to prove that each input results in the corresponding output when used in place of x in the equation $f(x) = 2x^2 - 1$. For example: $f(-2) = 2(-2)^2 - 1 = 8 - 1 = 7$, so $f(-2) = 7$.

4. Give students a copy of the **Input–Output Problems reproducible (page 30)**, and have them work individually or with a partner to solve each problem using their Input–Output Machines. You might choose to do the first word problem together. Monitor students' progress, and offer assistance as needed.

5. When students are finished, review the answers together. Invite volunteers to show how they solved each problem.

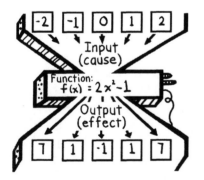

Input-Output Machines

Directions: Use these machines to solve the input–output problems.

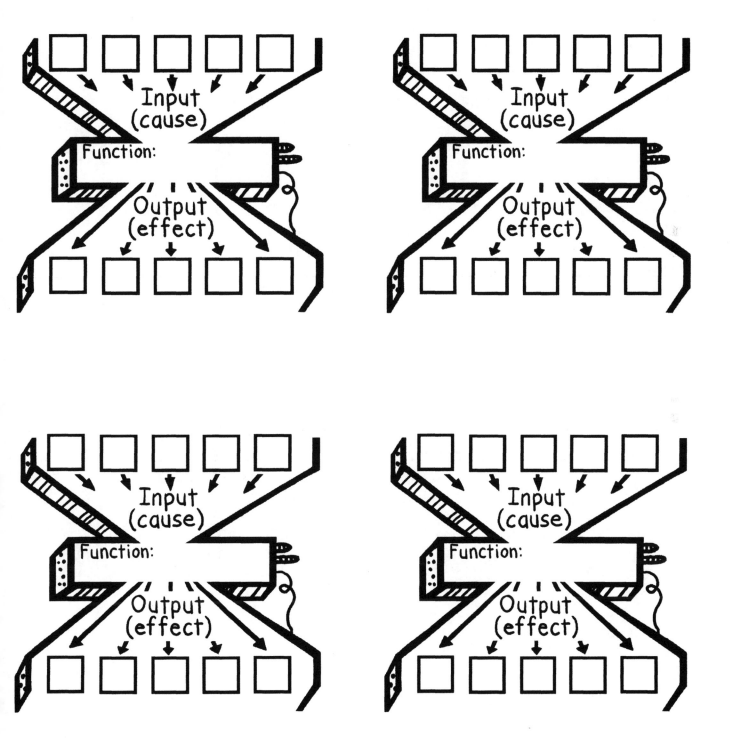

Input-Output Problems

Part A

Directions: Use the input-output machines to show the solution for each function. Complete each function rule, and write the missing numbers.

1. $f(x) = 2x^2 - 1$ Input: -2, -1, 0, 1, 2   Output: 7, 1, ____, ____, ____

2. $f(x) = 3x + 2$ Input: -2, -1, 0, 1, 2   Output: ____, ____, ____, ____, ____

3. $f(x) =$ ___$x + 2$ Input: -2, -1, 0, 1, 2   Output: -2, 0, 2, ____, ____

4. $f(x) =$ ___$x -$ ____   Input: -2, -1, 0, 1, ____   Output: -12, -7, -2, ____, 8

Part B

Directions: Use input-output machines to solve these problems.

5. In October, Tasty Taffy Apples are sold by mail order. It costs $10 for a package of three, plus $4 for shipping and handling. Write a function rule with variable x. Use the function rule to determine the cost for 2, 4, and 5 packages. Show the solution on an input-output machine.

6. Natasha has a cell phone through TalkSoMuch Phone Company. She pays $40 per month and can buy additional cool ring tones for $1.50 each. Write a function rule with variable x. Use the function rule to determine the cost for 3, 7, and 9 new ring tones. Show the solution on an input-output machine.

7. Jordan belongs to Buff It Up Gym. In order to join, he paid $100 introductory fee along with $60 per month. Write a function rule with variable x. Use the function rule to determine the cost of the gym after 3 months, 7 months, and 12 months. Show the solution on an input-output machine.

8. Write your own story problem involving a function rule. Show the solution on an input-output machine.

_____

_____

_____

_____

A Penny for Your Thoughts: Data Table

Skills Objectives
Describe, complete, and compare number patterns and sequences.
Distinguish between arithmetic and geometric sequences.
Use number patterns to make reasonable estimates.

Materials
Tables and
Sequences
reproducible

calculators

math journals or
writing paper

A **Data Table** can be used to evaluate sets or patterns of numbers. In this activity, students use a data table to organize and analyze different patterns of money and other numbers written in an arithmetic or geometric sequence.

1. Ask students: *Which do you think will give you more money in a month—a bank account that starts with $100 and increases by $50 daily or a bank account that starts with one penny and doubles daily?* Give students some thinking time, and then have them vote for their choice.

2. Give students a copy of the **Tables and Sequences reproducible (page 33)**, and display a copy to guide instruction. Explain to students that they can use a data table to help them organize and analyze each bank account's progress.

3. Work with students to complete the table of values for Days 1 to 10 for each account, as shown below. Ask: *Which account has more money after 10 days?* (the first account) *How much money do you think will be in each account after 20 days?* Invite students to share their estimates and explain their reasoning.

Day 1	Day 2	Day 3	Day 4	Day 5	Day 6	Day 7	Day 8	Day 9	Day 10
$100	$150	$200	$250	$300	$350	$400	$450	$500	$550
$0.01	$0.02	$0.04	$0.08	$0.16	$0.32	$0.64	$1.28	$2.56	$5.12

4. Continue for Days 11 to 20, using a calculator to complete the second table. Ask: *Which account has more money after 20 days?* (the penny account) *How much money is in each account?* ($1,050 in the first account; $5,242.88 in the penny account) *How much do you think will be in each account after 30 days?*

5. Have students complete the third table independently. Ask: *How much does each account have after 30 days? Which account is the better investment?* (The first account has $1,550; the penny account has $5,368,709.12, which is better.)

6. Explain to students that the two patterns of numbers in the data tables are examples of two different types of number sequences: an *arithmetic sequence,* in which each term after the first is a result of adding a fixed number or a common difference to the previous term; and a *geometric sequence,* in which each term after the first is a result of multiplying the previous term by a fixed number called the *common ratio.* Ask: *Which account shows an arithmetic sequence?* (the first account) *Which account shows a geometric sequence?* (the penny account)

7. Have students complete the table of sequences at the bottom of the reproducible. Do the first sequence together, and check for understanding before having students complete the rest on their own. Have student pairs compare their answers and recheck if they disagree. Then have them solve each other's number sequence.

Extended Learning

- Have students create their own story problem involving number sequences and use a data table to show the solution.

- Read aloud *One Grain of Rice* by Demi (Scholastic Press, 1997), and have students compare that story to the bank account problem they solved in class.

- Invite students to research and write about the Fibonacci number sequence.

Name _____ Date _____

Tables and Sequences

Directions: Follow your teacher's instructions to complete these tables.

Day 1	2	3	4	5	6	7	8	9	10
100	150	200	250	300	350	400	450	500	550
0.01	0.02	0.04	0.08	0.16	0.32	0.64	1.28	2.56	5.12

11	12	13	14	15	16	17	18	19	20
600	650	700	750	800	850	900	950	1,000	1,050
10.24	20.48	40.96	81.92	163.84	327.68	655.36	1,310.72	2,621.44	5,242.88

21	22	23	24	25	26	27	28	29	30
1,100	1,150	1,200	1,250	1,300	1,350	1,400	1,450	1,500	1,550

Complete this table. Tell whether the sequence in each row is arithmetic (A) or geometric (G). Write your own challenging number sequence in the last row.

								A or G
6	12	24	48	96	192	384	768	G
3	1	-1	-3	-5	-7	-9	-11	A
1	4	9	16	25	36	49	64	A
-2	8	-32	128	-512	2,048	-8,192	32,768	G
50	25	12.5	6.25	3.125	1.5625	0.78125	0.390625	G

Tables and Sequences

Directions: Follow your teacher's instructions to complete these tables.

Day 1	2	3	4	5	6	7	8	9	10

11	12	13	14	15	16	17	18	19	20

21	22	23	24	25	26	27	28	29	30

Complete this table. Tell whether the sequence in each row is arithmetic (A) or geometric (G). Write your own challenging number sequence in the last row.

									A or G
6	12	24	48						
3	1	–1	–3						
1	4	9	16						
–2	8	–32	128						
50	25	12.5	6.25						

Morph the Data: Relationship Map

Materials

Morph the Data reproducible

calculators

Skills Objectives

Write, solve, and graph algebraic equations that include two variables. Create and solve story problems involving algebraic relationships. Display and analyze different representations of mathematical information.

A **Relationship Map** shows different representations of the same mathematical information, giving students a big picture to help them solve a problem. For this activity, students create a relationship map consisting of a narrative summary, an algebraic equation, a data table, and a linear graph to help them solve story problems with two variables.

1. Display the following story problem on the board, and read it aloud. Invite volunteers to underline the important parts.

   Erin is a competitive swimmer, keeping in shape for an Olympic swim meet. She burns approximately 10 calories per minute swimming freestyle, and 8 calories per minute swimming backstroke. If she wants to burn 1,000 calories a day swimming laps, what are some possible ways she can accomplish her goal using a combination of freestyle and backstroke?

2. Give students a copy of the **Morph the Data reproducible (page 36)**, and display a copy to guide instruction. Explain to students that they can use a relationship map to help them organize and solve the problem. Start with the box labeled *Word Problem*. Work together to summarize the important facts needed to solve the problem. For example:

   Erin burns 10 cal/min swimming freestyle.
   She burns 8 cal/min swimming backstroke.
   What possible combinations equal a total of 1,000 calories?

3. Ask students to suggest a linear equation for the problem that includes variables x and y, where x represents the minutes of freestyle swimming and y represents the minutes of backstroke swimming. Have students write the correct equation in the box labeled *Equation*. *(10x + 8y = 1,000)*

4. Distribute calculators, and work together to complete the box labeled *Table* for the linear equation, choosing values for x and solving for the corresponding y. Include at least five pairs of values, and demonstrate how to plug each value of x into the equation to solve for y. For example, if the values of x (freestyle) are *10, 20, 30, 40,* and *50,* the values of y (backstroke) are *112.5, 100, 87.5, 75,* and *62.5.*

5. Finally, work together to graph the linear equation, plotting each pair of x and y values on the coordinate grid in the box labeled *Graph*. Remind students to write a number scale on the x-axis and y-axis that includes all the values from the table. Invite volunteers to help plot and connect the points to show the line graph.

6. Give each student another copy of the reproducible, and divide the class into groups of four. Instruct students to each write a word problem and then repeatedly rotate their papers so each group member completes a different part of each other's map. Tell students to check the prior work done before they complete the next section of each map.

7. Display the completed maps to create an interactive bulletin board. Add flip-up covers on the boxes labeled *Equation*, *Table*, and *Graph* to make the display interactive.

Extended Learning

Present a word problem that involves two linear equations, and have students use a different color to graph each equation on the same coordinate grid. You might also have students write and solve their own double-equation problems.

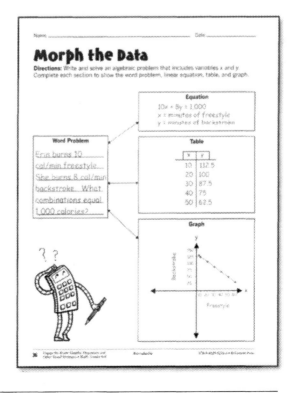

Name _____   Date _____

Morph the Data

Directions: Write and solve an algebraic problem that includes variables *x* and *y*. Complete each section to show the word problem, linear equation, table, and graph.

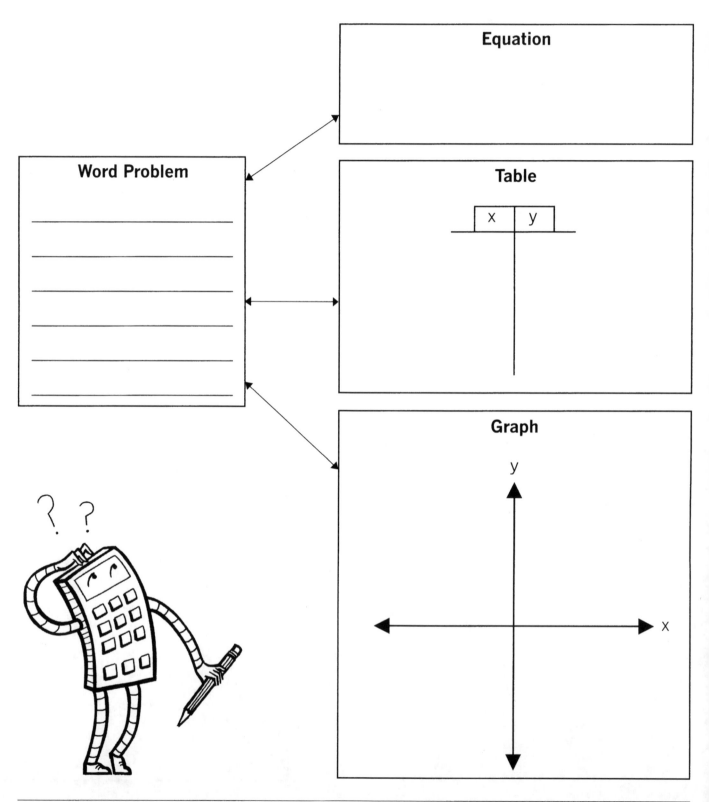

Engage the Brain: Graphic Organizers and Other Visual Strategies • Math, Grades 6–8   Reproducible   978-1-4129-5231-6 • © Corwin Press

Inequality Match: Group Organizer

Skills Objectives
Identify, solve, graph, and sort inequalities using >, < , ≥ , and ≤.
Use mathematical models to represent and understand quantitative
relationships.

In this activity, students sort and solve inequalities by using a
Group Organizer in the form of open-mouthed alligators representing
the symbols >, < , ≥ , and ≤. The alligators show sets of matching
inequalities that include written statements, symbolic expressions,
solutions, and number-line graphs of those solutions.

1. Ahead of time, copy and cut apart a set of **Inequality Cards**
   (page 39) for each group of two or four students. Store each set of
   cards in a resealable plastic bag.

2. Write the following problem on the board, and read it aloud to
   students: *Suppose you want to earn an average of at least 80*
   points to get a B in this class. So far you have scored an 81, 75,
   and 78 on your first three tests. What must you score on your next
   test to earn a B or better?

3. To solve the problem, tell students that they need to write and
   solve an inequality. Review the symbols and rules for solving
   inequalities >, < , ≥ , and ≤. Remind students that when they
   multiply or divide each side of an inequality by a negative number,
   they should reverse the inequality symbol. Also demonstrate how
   to graph each type of inequality on a number line, showing an
   open ray (open-circle endpoint) for graphs of > or < and a closed
   ray (solid endpoint) for graphs of ≥ or ≤.

4. Divide the class into groups of two or four students, and have each
   group work together to solve the problem, writing the inequality,
   solving for variable *x*, and graphing the solution. Offer assistance

as needed. Invite each group to show their solution on the board. Then display the answers: $(81 + 75 + 78 + x) \div 4 \geq 80$, so $x \geq 86$.

And

$x \geq 86$

0   10   20   30   40   50   60   70   80   90   100

5. Give each group a bag of inequality cards to sort into sets of four. Each set includes the inequality written in words, the inequality written as a number sentence, the solution for the inequality (solving for the variable), and a number line graph of that solution. Provide the answers for one set of cards as an example.

6. Give each group two copies of the **Gator Sorter reproducible (page 40)**, and tell them to sort their card sets according to the inequality symbol used in the solution. Have them glue the < sets in the first alligator, the > sets in the second alligator, the ≤ sets in the third alligator, and the ≥ sets in the fourth alligator. Tell them to label each alligator with its inequality symbol. (Point out that the mouths of the alligators resemble the inequality symbols; the open mouth always faces the larger value.)

7. Invite each group to share their results and explain how they sorted their cards.

Extended Learning

Challenge students to graph compound inequalities, such as $x > 5$ and $x \leq 7$ or $y \leq -4$ or $y > 4$. Tell them to graph each pair on the same number line.

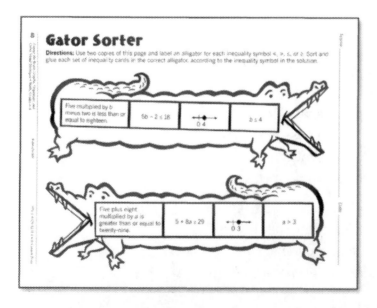

Inequality Cards

Written Inequality	Inequality	Number Line	Solution ✂
Two multiplied by x less four is less than or equal to ten.	$2x - 4 \leq 10$	0 7	$x \leq 7$
Eight plus five multiplied by a is less than eighteen.	$8 + 5a < 18$	0 2	$a < 2$
Three multiplied by x minus nine is greater than twelve.	$3x - 9 > 12$	0 7	$x > 7$
Five plus eight multiplied by a is greater than or equal to twenty-nine.	$5 + 8a \geq 29$	0 3	$a > 3$
Five multiplied by b minus two is less than or equal to eighteen.	$5b - 2 \leq 18$	0 4	$b \leq 4$
One third multiplied by b plus six is greater than negative six.	$\frac{1}{3} b + 6 > -6$	−36	$b > -36$
Negative nine multiplied by a is greater than sixty-three.	$-9a > 63$	-7 0	$a < -7$
The sum of eleven and thirteen is greater than or equal to six multiplied by x minus six.	$11 + 13 \geq 6x - 6$	0 5	$x \leq 5$

Gator Sorter

Directions: Use two copies of this page, and label an alligator for each inequality symbol <, >, ≤, or ≥. Sort and glue each set of inequality cards in the correct alligator according to the inequality symbol in the solution.

Shrink and Simplify: Box Flowchart

Skills Objectives
Simplify and solve multistep algebraic equations.
Use mathematical models to represent and understand quantitative relationships.

Materials
Shrink and Simplify reproducible

math journals

A **Box Flowchart** offers students a visual layout of a step-by-step process, such as simplifying and solving algebraic equations. By using a flowchart of boxes that decrease in size, students visually see how each step reduces to the final answer.

1. Write the following one- and two-step algebraic equations on the board:

   $\square + 2 = 14$

   $m + 2 = 14$

   $4m + 2 = 14$

   Point out to students that the first example uses a box to represent an unknown value, whereas the other two examples use the variable m.

2. Demonstrate how to solve for the variable (unknown value) by using opposite operations to isolate the variable. Remind students that whatever they do to one side of the equation they must also do to the other. Point out that the solutions for all three examples start off the same way but the third example continues.

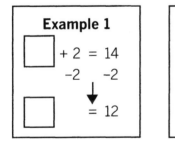

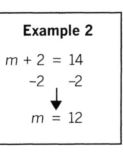

Example 1

$\square + 2 = 14$

$-2 \quad -2$

$\downarrow$

$\square = 12$

Example 2

$m + 2 = 14$

$-2 \quad -2$

$\downarrow$

$m = 12$

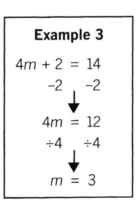

Example 3

$4m + 2 = 14$

$-2 \quad -2$

$\downarrow$

$4m = 12$

$\div 4 \quad \div 4$

$\downarrow$

$m = 3$

3. Give students a copy of the **Shrink and Simplify reproducible (page 43)**, and display a copy to guide instruction. Have students write the equation $m + 3m - 2 + 3(2m + 1) = 21$ on the *Start* line. Explain that they can use the box flowchart to help them solve the equation step by step, simplifying and reducing the equation until the variable is alone on one side.

4. Point out the first box, and explain that the first step is to *Use the Distributive Property*. Demonstrate how to use the distributive property to remove the parentheses from the equation. Remind students that each term inside the parentheses gets multiplied by the number in front of the parentheses.

$$m + 3m - 2 + \mathbf{3(2m + 1)} = 21$$

$$m + 3m - 2 + \mathbf{6m + 3} = 21$$

5. Next, demonstrate how to *Combine Like Terms* in the second box. Remind students that *like terms* are those that have the same variable, such as *m*.

$$\mathbf{m + 3m} - 2 + 6m + 3 = 21$$

$$\mathbf{4m} - 2 + \mathbf{6m} + 3 = 21$$

$$\mathbf{10m} - 2 + 3 = 21$$

6. For the third box, show students how to *Undo Addition and Subtraction* one term at a time. Remind students to use the opposite operation to get rid of the terms on each side of the variable and to do the same calculation on both sides.

$$10m - 2 + \mathbf{3} = 21$$
$$ \mathbf{-3} \quad \mathbf{-3}$$
$$10m - \mathbf{2} = 18$$
$$ \mathbf{+2} \quad \mathbf{+2}$$
$$10m = 20$$

7. Then complete the last box, *Undo Multiplication and Division*.

$$\mathbf{10}m = 20$$
$$\mathbf{\div 10} \quad \mathbf{\div 10}$$
$$m = 2$$

8. Check that students understand how to use the flowchart. Then have students work independently to solve other equations such as:

$3(2n + 5) = -39$

$k + 2(4k - 3) = 12$

$6(1/3g + 1/2) + 9 = 28$

(Answers: $n = -9$, $k = 2$, $g = 8$)

Name _____ Date _____

Shrink and Simplify

Directions: Use this flowchart to solve equations step-by-step.

Equation: m+3m-2+3(2m+1)=21

Use the Distributive Property
m+3m-2+3(2m+1)=21
m+3m-2+6m+3=21

Combine Like Terms
m+3m-2+6m+3=21
4m-2+6m+3=21
10m-2+3=21

Undo Addition and Subtraction
10m-2+3=21
10m-2=18
10m=20

Undo Multiplication and Division
10m=20
m=2

Answer
m=2

Name _____ Date _____

Shrink and Simplify

Directions: Use this flowchart to solve equations step-by-step.

Equation: _____

> **Use the Distributive Property**

> **Combine Like Terms**

> **Undo Addition and Subtraction**

> **Undo Multiplication and Division**

> **Answer**

CHAPTER 3

Geometry

Three's a 180° Crowd: Concept Map

Skills Objectives

Identify, describe, classify, and compare different types of triangles. Draw different types of triangles using a protractor.

A **Concept Map** is an outline of key concepts for a particular topic, such as the classification of triangles. It creates a hierarchical arrangement of information, starting with a broad definition and leading to specific details. Concept maps are an excellent tool for organizing categories and subcategories of information.

Materials

Triangle Concept Map reproducible

protractors

drawing paper

1. Ask the class to brainstorm what they know about triangles, and list their ideas on the board. Explain to students that they can make a concept map to help them organize and classify information about different types of triangles.

"A cute" equilateral triangle

2. Distribute enlarged copies of the **Triangle Concept Map reproducible (page 46)** to students, and display a copy to guide instruction. In the top triangle, have students write a complete definition of a triangle. For example: *A three-sided polygon with three angles that total 180°.*

3. Ask students: *What are the two main ways to classify triangles?* Have them write the answers *Sides* and *Angles* in the next two triangles of the concept map.

4. Review with students the meaning of *congruent* (same shape and size). Ask: *How many congruent sides can a triangle have?* As a clue, point out the shapes of the three triangles just below the *Sides* label, and have students write the answers in those three triangles. (*0 congruent sides, 2 congruent sides, 3 congruent*

sides) Then show students how to draw matching tick marks in the congruent sides.

5. Refer students back to the *Angles* label. Ask: *What three types of angles can a triangle have? How many of those angles does a triangle need in order to be classified by the name of that angle?* As a clue, point out the shapes of the three triangles just below the *Angles* label. Have students write the answers in those three triangles. *(1 right angle, 1 obtuse angle, 3 acute angles)*

6. For the last row of triangles, have students write the names of the corresponding triangles that go with each description. *(Sides: Scalene Triangle, Isosceles Triangle, Equilateral Triangle. Angles: Right Triangle, Obtuse Triangle, Acute Triangle.)* Point out that a triangle can be identified by both its sides and its angles combined, such as a *right isosceles triangle.*

7. Instruct students to use a protractor to draw each type of triangle listed on their concept map. Suggest that they draw a design or pattern of triangles of different sizes, shapes, and colors, including congruent triangles and similar triangles (same shape, different size). Have them write the name of each triangle and the lengths of its sides in their drawing. Remind them to draw tick marks to show congruent sides.

8. Initiate a discussion with students by asking questions such as: *Can you make a triangle with more than one obtuse angle?* (no) *Can you make a triangle with more than one right angle?* (no) *Can a right triangle be equilateral?* (no) *Can an acute triangle be scalene?* (yes) *Can an obtuse triangle be equilateral?* (no) *Can an obtuse triangle be isosceles?* (yes) *What do you notice about the angles of an isosceles or equilateral triangle?* (the opposite angles of congruent sides are also congruent)

Extended Learning

- Have students use geoboards to show each type of triangle.

- Have students create a similar concept map for quadrilaterals.

- Ask students to explore triangles more in depth by answering these questions: *How many lines of symmetry does each type of triangle have? How many diagonals does each type of triangle have?*

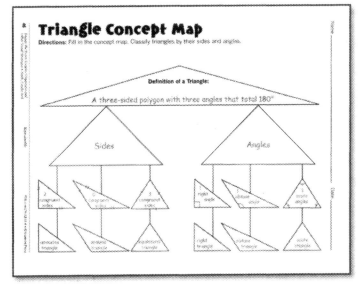

Triangle Concept Map

Directions: Fill in the concept map. Classify triangles by their sides and angles.

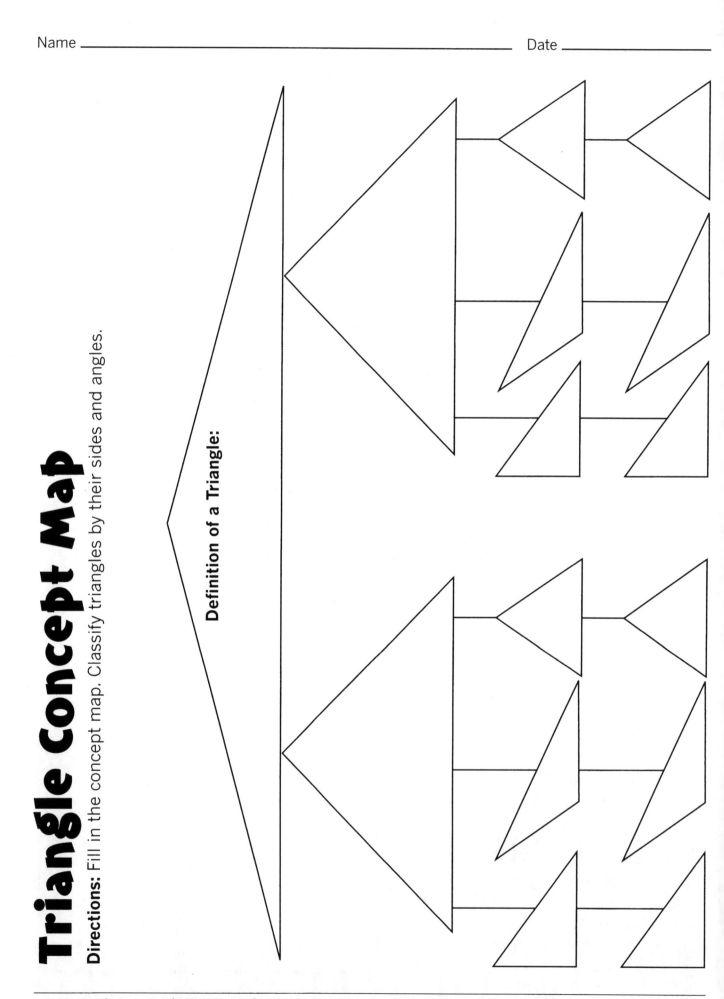

Definition of a Triangle:

Engage the Brain: Graphic Organizers and Other Visual Strategies • Math, Grades 6–8   *Reproducible*   978-1-4129-5231-6 • © Corwin Press

Polygon Perspective: Word Web

Skills Objectives
Identify, classify, and compare polygons.
Use word parts (prefixes, suffixes) to compare similar terms and definitions.

A **Word Web** is a network of terms, definitions, descriptions, and examples that are all connected to a topic in the center of the web. It is a useful tool for brainstorming ideas and assessing knowledge of a topic. In this activity, students create a word web as a warm-up for a more in-depth investigation of polygons.

1. Divide the class into small groups, and give each group a sheet of butcher paper and some markers. Review on the board how to create a word web, writing the topic in the center and branching off with descriptive words and phrases as shown in the example below. Then, when you say *Go,* have groups race to complete a word web about polygons. Give them five minutes to complete their webs. Suggest that they include descriptive words, definitions, and categories of polygons.

2. Collect the word webs, and post them in front of the class to compare and contrast. Point out the similarities and differences. Discuss the meanings of terms such as *regular polygon, irregular polygon, concave, convex,* and *vertices.*

3. Give students a copy of the **Polygon Perspective reproducible (page 49)** to complete individually or in groups. Offer guidance as needed. Have them use a dictionary to look up words that begin with the same prefixes, such as *tri, poly, penta,* or *hexa.* You might also have them write definitions and sample sentences for the words in their math journals.

4. Display a copy of the Polygon Perspective reproducible, and invite volunteers to write each name and prefix. Explain that the common suffix –*gon* means "shape with angles," and each prefix tells how many angles are in that shape. Note that *polygon* means "many angles." Then have students name and discuss other words that begin with each prefix, such as *tricycle* and *trisect.*

Materials
Polygon Perspective reproducible

Quadrilateral Corner reproducible

Polygon Print reproducible

butcher paper or chart paper

markers and colored pencils

dictionaries

math journals

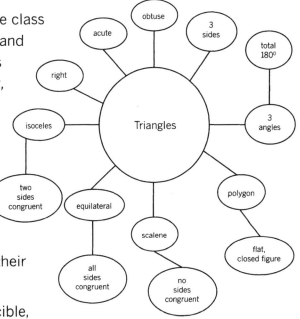

5. Give students a copy of the **Quadrilateral Corner reproducible (page 50)**, and display a copy to guide instruction. Explain that there are many types of quadrilaterals and some belong to more than one category. For example, a square is also a parallelogram and a rectangle, but the most specific name is *square*. (To clarify, refer to dog classifications. For example, a Chihuahua can be called an *animal* or *toy dog*, but the most specific name is *Chihuahua*.)

6. Show an example of each kind of quadrilateral, including tick and angle marks to show congruent sides and right angles. Then have students work independently to complete the page. Review the answers, and ask students to correct their work as needed.

7. Have students complete a **Polygon Print reproducible (page 51)** to show what they've learned, outlining as many different shapes as possible to fill the page. You might also have them use a second copy to draw a tessellating pattern of shapes (an alternating pattern without gaps or overlaps, like tiles on a floor).

8. Display students' artwork around the room to create a geometric art gallery.

Extended Learning

- Provide students with pattern blocks to create tessellating patterns.

- Invite students to explore tangram puzzles and use them to create patterns and pictures. (You can find many printouts online using any search engine.)

Polygon Perspective

Directions: Complete this chart about polygons.

# of Sides or Vertices	Polygon Name	Prefix	Words with the Same Prefix
3	triangle	tri	tricycle, trisect
4	quadrilateral	quad	quadricep, quadratic
5	pentagon	penta	pentathlon, pentameter
6	hexagon	hexa	hexad, hexagram
7	heptagon	hepta	heptarchy, heptathlon
8	octagon	octa	octavo, octane
9	nonagon	nona	nonagenarian, nonappearance
10	decagon	deca	decade, decameter

Quadrilateral Corner

Directions: Draw a picture and write a description of each quadrilateral.

Parallelogram

A parallelogram is a quadrilateral with opposite sides parallel and equal.

Rectangle

A rectangle is a parallelogram with four right angles.

Square

A square is a rectangle with four equal sides. It is also a type of rhombus.

Rhombus

A rhombus is a parallelogram with four equal sides.

A **trapezoid** is another type of quadrilateral. How is it different from the other four quadrilaterals? Write a description and draw a picture of a trapezoid.

A trapezoid has only one pair of parallel sides. It is a quadrilateral but not a parallelogram.

Polygon Perspective

Directions: Complete this chart about polygons.

# of Sides or Vertices	Polygon Name	Prefix	Words with the Same Prefix
3			
4			
5			
6			
7			
8			
9			
10			

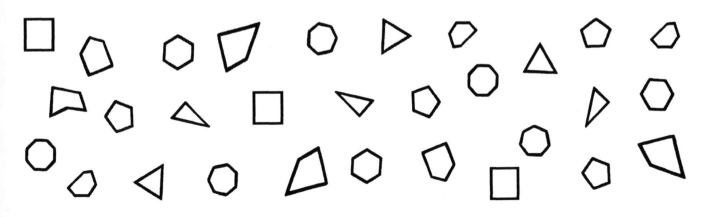

Quadrilateral Corner

Directions: Draw a picture and write a description of each quadrilateral.

Parallelogram	Rectangle
_____ _____ _____	_____ _____ _____

Square	Rhombus
_____ _____	_____ _____

A **trapezoid** is another type of quadrilateral. How is it different from the other four quadrilaterals? Write a description and draw a picture of a trapezoid.

_____
_____
_____

 Engage the Brain: Graphic Organizers and Other Visual Strategies • Math, Grades 6–8   *Reproducible*   978-1-4129-5231-6 • © Corwin Press

Polygon Print

Directions: Outline the following polygons in any size or orientation. Label each one with its corresponding number.

1. equilateral triangle   **5.** rhombus   **9.** hexagon

2. right triangle   **6.** rectangle   **10.** heptagon

3. isosceles triangle   **7.** trapezoid   **11.** octagon

4. scalene triangle   **8.** pentagon   **12.** decagon

Diagonal Division: Picture Model

Skills Objectives

Find the total degrees of the interior angles of a polygon by drawing its diagonals.

Write a formula for finding the total degrees of a polygon with *n* sides. Use geometric modeling to solve problems.

Using a **Picture Model** can help students visualize geometric figures and manipulate shapes mentally and on paper. The visual representation can also help students identify patterns and relationships. In this activity, students use picture models to explore the use of diagonals as well as the relationship between triangles formed by diagonals and the total degrees of a polygon's interior angles.

Materials

Polygon Shapes reproducible

Diagonal Division Table reproducible

scissors

rulers

colored pencils

1. Give students a copy of the **Polygon Shapes reproducible (page 54)**, and display a copy to guide instruction. Ask students to name and describe each polygon. Suggest that they mark each side as they count to identify each shape. Remind students that each polygon has the same number of sides and angles.

2. Have students draw a large dot in each angle of the triangle. Remind them that the sum of the measure of the angles of a triangle is always 180°. Ask: *How can we prove that the angles add up to 180° without using a measuring tool?* Explain that 180° is a straight line. Have students cut out their triangle, cut off the three angles, and place the dotted angles edge to edge to prove that they form a straight line along the bottom.

3. Then ask: *How can we determine the sum of the angles of the other polygons without using a measuring tool?* Tell students that

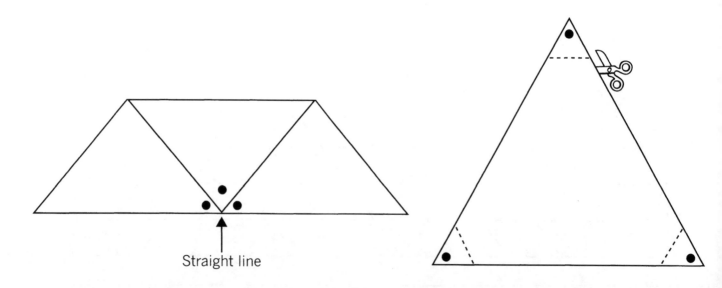

Straight line

by drawing diagonals to divide each shape into triangles, they can determine the sum of the angles. Explain that a *diagonal* is a line segment connecting one vertex to another that is not next to it.

4. Use a ruler to demonstrate how to draw a diagonal for a quadrilateral. Explain that all diagonals should be drawn from one vertex only. Ask: *How many diagonals can we draw for a quadrilateral?* (one) *How many triangles are formed when we draw that diagonal?* (two) *How can we use those two triangles to figure out the sum of the angles of a quadrilateral?* (multiply 180° by 2)

5. Have students draw the diagonal for their quadrilateral and draw dots in all the angles, using a different color for each triangle. Have them cut apart the two triangles, cut off both sets of three angles, and put together each set to prove that the total is 2 x 180° = 360°.

6. Give students a copy of the **Diagonal Division Table reproducible (page 55)** to record their results. Use a copy to guide instruction. Show students how to complete the first two rows of the table. Make sure they understand that the *Number of Triangles Formed* refers to the number of triangles formed by drawing all of the diagonals.

7. Work together to complete the answers for a pentagon. Ask: *How many triangles are formed by drawing all the diagonals of a pentagon?* (three) *How can we use those three triangles to find the sum of the angles of a pentagon?* (multiply 180° by 3 = 540°)

8. Have students complete the rest of the table on their own. For the *n-gon,* tell students they need to look for a pattern in their answers in the chart to figure out a formula for finding the sum of the angles of a polygon with *n* sides.

9. Invite students to share and explain their answers. For the *n-gon,* point out the pattern of answers showing that *n* – 2 triangles are formed, so the formula is (*n* – 2) x 180°. For the bottom set of answers, remind students that the angles of a regular polygon are all equal, so the measure of one angle is the total sum divided by the total number of angles. Then have students apply their knowledge by answering questions such as: *What is the total number of degrees of a dodecagon, a 12-sided polygon?* (1,800°)

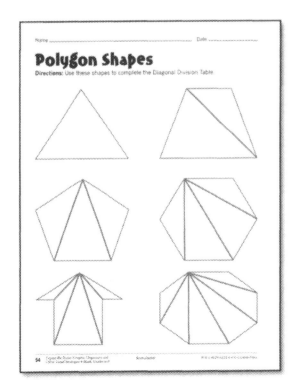

Polygon Shapes

Directions: Use these shapes to complete the Diagonal Division Table.

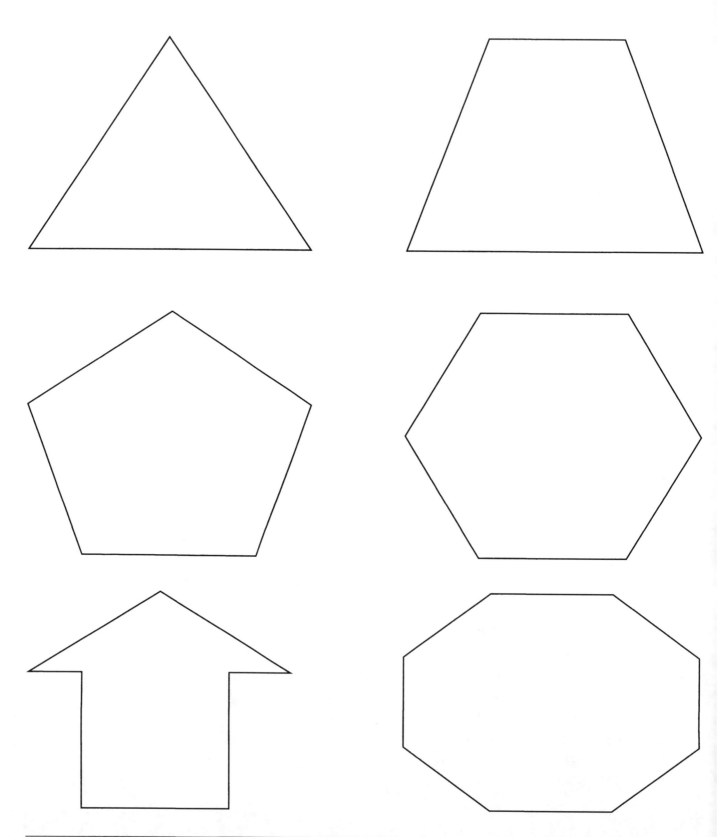

 Engage the Brain: Graphic Organizers and Other Visual Strategies • Math, Grades 6–8   *Reproducible*   978-1-4129-5231-6 • © Corwin Press

Diagonal Division Table

Directions: Use the polygon shapes to help you complete this table. For each polygon, draw all the diagonals from a single vertex. Count the number of triangles formed. Then calculate the total degrees of all the angles in the polygon. Use your results to figure out the formula for the total degrees of an *n*-gon.

Polygon	Number of Sides of the Polygon	Number of Triangles Formed	Total Degrees of All Angles in the Polygon
Triangle			1 triangle x (180°) = 180
Quadrilateral			
Pentagon			
Hexagon			
Heptagon			
Octagon			
***n*-gon**	*n*		

If all the polygons are regular polygons, what is the measure of each angle in the polygon?

Triangle: _____   Pentagon: _____   Heptagon: _____

Quadrilateral: _____   Hexagon: _____   Octagon: _____

Shape Translations: Coordinate Map

Materials

Coordinate Graph Guide reproducible

Shape Translations reproducible

chart paper

pushpins

large rubber bands or yarn

colored pencils

rulers

Skills Objectives

Use coordinate geometry to graph shapes on a coordinate plane. Identify and plot geometric figure translations on a coordinate plane. Use geometric modeling to solve problems.

A **Coordinate Map** is a visual tool used both in mathematics and in social studies to show the coordinates or the location of objects on a coordinate plane. In this activity, students use a coordinate map to show the location of geometric figures and to translate, or slide, those figures to new locations on the coordinate plane.

1. Make a large, four-quadrant coordinate graph on chart paper, and post it on a bulletin board in front of the class. Save it for later in the activity.

2. Begin the lesson by drawing a triangle on the board and labeling the vertices A(2,4), B(–4,–2), C(4,–2). Ask students: *What have I drawn?* (a triangle) *What have I written at the vertices of the triangle?* (ordered pairs, coordinate pairs) *What do you think we're going to do with this triangle?* (graph it) *How do you think we're going to translate the triangle?* Tell students that they will learn the answer to the last question by completing the activity.

3. Give students a copy of the **Coordinate Graph Guide reproducible (page 59)**. Explain that they are going to learn how to graph and locate different shapes on a coordinate plane. Use your large coordinate graph to review the following parts as students label those parts on their reproducible: *x-axis, y-axis, origin, Quadrant I (+,+), Quadrant II (–,+), Quadrant III (–,–), Quadrant IV (+,–).*

4. Refer back to the triangle to demonstrate how to graph on a coordinate plane. Explain that the first number in any ordered pair is the *x-coordinate* and the second number is the *y-coordinate.* Show students how to graph the coordinate *(2,4)* for the top of the triangle, showing how to "go out, then up." You may want to use the analogy: *You must walk to the tree → before you can climb it ↑.* Use a pushpin to mark the spot on your coordinate graph. Repeat the process for the two other coordinates B(–4,–2) and C(4,–2).

5. Explain that when the *x*-coordinate is positive, go right; when *x* is negative, go left. When the *y*-coordinate is positive, go up; when *y* is negative, go down. Invite volunteers to use the same-colored pushpins to mark the coordinates on the large graph. Then use

a rubber band or yarn around the three pushpins to show the triangle. Give students time to copy the process on their own paper, and write how to graph coordinates step-by-step.

6. Give students a copy of the **Shape Translations reproducible (page 60)**, and explain the process of *translation*—"sliding" a shape to a new position on the same coordinate plane. Write the following example on the board, and explain that the translation equation tells how much to add or subtract to each *x* or *y* value for each pair. The same amount of *x* or *y* is added to each original value so the exact same shape is shown in a new location. Point out that the new translated values for *A, B, C* are marked *A´, B´, C´*.

   Original Positions: *A*(2,4), *B*(−4,−2), *C*(4,−2)

   Translation: $(x,y) \rightarrow (x + 3, y - 1)$

   New Positions: *A´*(5,3), *B´*(−1,−3), *C´*(7,−3)

7. Use two different colors to demonstrate how to graph the original and translated values on the same coordinate graph. Have students do the same on their first coordinate graph. Use a rubber band or yarn to show the translated triangle on your large graph. Point out that the translated shape is only a slide from the original, not a turn or a flip (neither a rotation nor a reflection).

8. Have students lightly color their two triangles. Ask: *What do you think we'll see if we draw line segments connecting the matching vertices of the two triangles together, such as connecting point A(2,4) to point A´(5,3)?* Connect the pairs of vertices to show students the answer. *(a three-dimensional figure of a triangular prism)* Have students do the same on their coordinate graph.

9. Have students graph the following shapes and translations on the three remaining coordinate graphs. Tell them to join the pairs of vertices together to draw the three-dimensional figures. Monitor students as they work, and offer assistance as needed. Encourage them to refer to their Coordinate Graph Guide and the example on display.

Original Positions

Triangle (3,–2), (0,–5), (6,–5)

Quadrilateral (2,2), (5,2), (2,4), (5,4)

Pentagon (–3,–2), (–4,–3), (–4,–4), (–2,–4), (–2,–3)

Translations

Triangle: *Translation* $(x,y) \rightarrow (x - 2, y + 1)$

Quadrilateral: *Translation* $(x,y) \rightarrow (x - 2, y - 3)$

Pentagon: *Translation* $(x,y) \rightarrow (x + 4, y + 2)$

10. Invite students to share and compare their results. Ask them to explain how they graphed their coordinate points and how they figured out the translated values. Have them identify each three-dimensional figure and its faces.

Extended Learning

- Provide corkboard for students to create their own pushpin coordinate grids for modeling how to graph and translate shapes on a coordinate plane.

- Encourage students to explore other kinds of *transformations* (changes in position or size), including reflection and rotation on a coordinate plane.

- Have students use coordinate geometry to identify locations on a road map, such as *(E,4)*, or identify latitude and longitude, such as *(+30° latitude, +98° longitude)*.

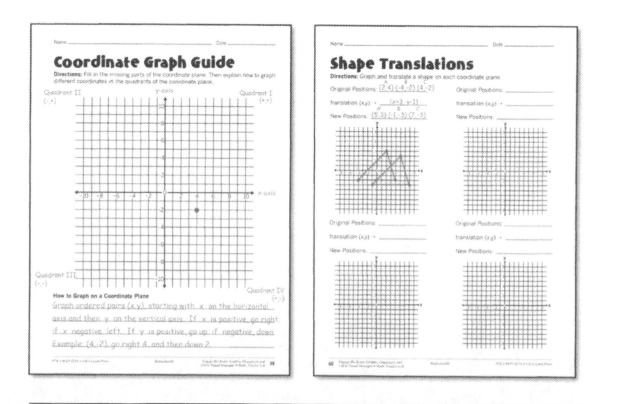

Coordinate Graph Guide

Directions: Fill in the missing parts of the coordinate plane. Then explain how to graph different coordinates in the quadrants of the coordinate plane.

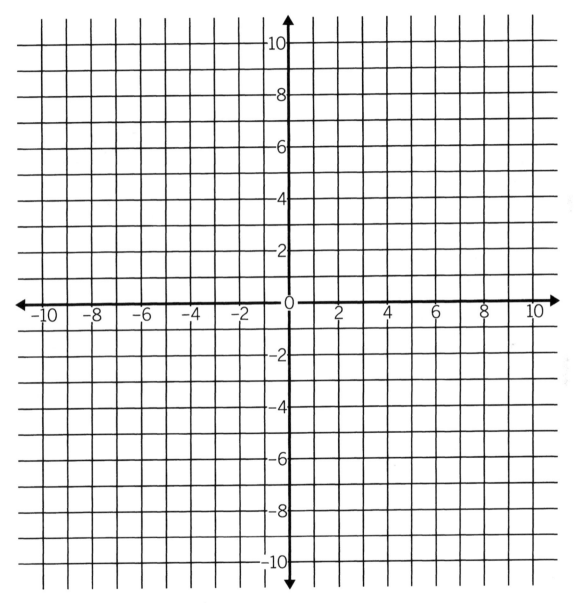

How to Graph on a Coordinate Plane

_____

_____

_____

_____

Shape Translations

Directions: Graph and translate a shape on each coordinate plane.

Original Positions: _____

translation (x,y) → _____

New Positions: _____

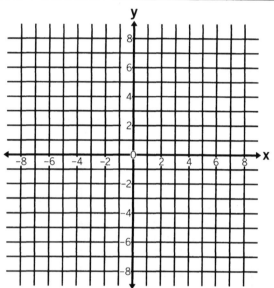

Original Positions: _____

translation (x,y) → _____

New Positions: _____

Original Positions: _____

translation (x,y) → _____

New Positions: _____

Original Positions: _____

translation (x,y) → _____

New Positions: _____

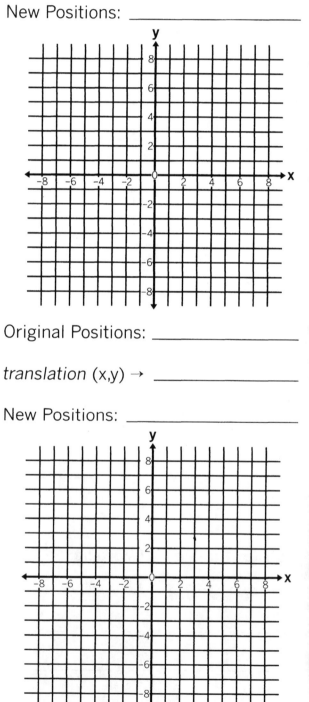

Spotlight on Students: Circle Graph

Skills Objectives

Calculate, measure, and draw parts of a circle graph.
Draw and describe circles in a design.

A **Circle Graph**, also called a pie graph, is a quick, visual way to compare parts of a whole. In this activity, students use their knowledge of circles to create a circle graph and a flag showing a "circle of learning" at their school.

1. Display on the board the number of students in each grade level at your school. Explain to students that they will be making a circle graph of that information.

2. Give students a calculator, a protractor, and a copy of the **Spotlight on Students reproducible (page 63)**. Set up a chart on the board, and work with students to calculate the degrees for each section of the circle graph, multiplying the fraction of students per grade level by 360° (the degrees of a whole circle). Have students copy and complete the chart in their math journals. For example:

Number	Fraction of All Students	Degrees of a Circle
6th graders: 120	$\frac{120}{420} = \frac{24}{84} = \frac{2}{7}$	$\frac{2}{7}$ x 360° = 103°
7th graders: 175	$\frac{175}{420} = \frac{35}{84} = \frac{5}{12}$	$\frac{5}{12}$ x 360° = 150°
8th graders: 125	$\frac{125}{420} = \frac{25}{84}$	$\frac{25}{84}$ x 360° = 107°

3. Then draw a circle on the board, or display a copy of the Spotlight on Students reproducible. Use a protractor to demonstrate how to measure and draw each part of the graph as students follow along on their own circles. Use exact values or use rounded values to the nearest five or ten degrees (e.g., 100°, 150°, and 110°).

4. Ask students questions about their completed circle graph, such as: *What does your circle graph show at a glance?* (the relative size of each grade level) *Which grade level has the most students? Which grade level has the fewest students?*

5. Tell students they will be using their knowledge of circles to design a school flag representing "a circle of learning" as described at the bottom of the reproducible. Read the directions aloud, and check for understanding before having students work individually or with a partner to complete the activity.

6. If needed, review with students the parts of a circle (radius, diameter, center, chord, arc) and how to use a compass. You might also allow students the option of using a computer program to design and draw their flag.

7. Invite students to share their results. Have them explain how they measured and drew each circle (such as circles *b* and *f*) and how they created their design.

Extended Learning

- Have students conduct a school survey and make a circle graph of their results.

- Have students calculate the circumference and area of the circles in their flag.

- Discuss the meaning of *pi* (π), the constant ratio of any circle's circumference to its diameter that results in an endless decimal rounded to 3.14. Have students explore that relationship by measuring circular objects such as the lids of canned foods, measuring the circumference of the can, and dividing by the diameter to get the ratio *c/d* (which should always be ~3.14).

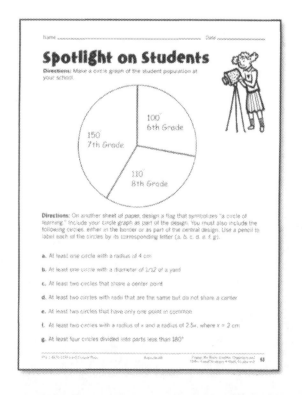

Spotlight on Students

Directions: Make a circle graph of the student population at your school.

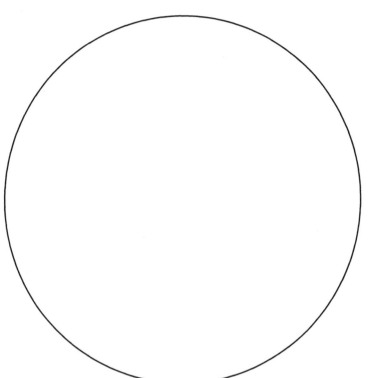

Directions: On another sheet of paper, design a flag that symbolizes "a circle of learning." Include your circle graph as part of the design. You must also include the following circles, either in the border or as part of the central design. Use a pencil to label each of the circles by its corresponding letter (*a, b, c, d, e, f, g*).

a. At least one circle with a radius of 4 cm

b. At least one circle with a diameter of 1/12 of a yard

c. At least two circles that share a center point

d. At least two circles with radii that are the same but do not share a center

e. At least two circles that have only one point in common

f. At least two circles with a radius of *x* and a radius of 2.5*x*, where *x* = 2 cm

g. At least four circles divided into parts less than 180°

CHAPTER 4

Measurement

Size It Up: Compare and Contrast Chart

Skills Objectives

Identify, compare, and convert customary and metric units of measure. Sort and classify units of measure.

A **Compare and Contrast Chart** is used to show similarities and differences. In this activity, students create and use a compare and contrast chart to categorize and compare customary and metric units of length, weight, and capacity.

Materials

Size It Up reproducible

Conversion Cards reproducible

scratch paper or math journals

scissors

glue

1. Read the following definitions aloud, and ask students to secretly write the word or term they think is being defined: *the distance between two points* (length); *the amount a container can hold* (capacity); *the heaviness of something* (weight); *the main system of measurement used in the United States* (customary system); *the main system of measurement used in Europe and most other countries* (metric system). Read the answers aloud for students to self-check. Ask: *What do you think we're going to study today?* (types of measurements)

2. Give each student three copies of the **Size It Up reproducible (page 66)** and one copy of the **Conversion Cards reproducible (page 67)**. Explain to

students that they will be making three different charts to compare and contrast customary and metric units of measure. Ask: *What three main categories of measure did we just define?* Have them write *Length, Weight/Mass,* or *Capacity* at the top of separate Size It Up reproducibles.

3. Tell students to decide which conversion cards to put in each box of each chart—the box labeled *Customary,* the box labeled *Metric,* or the box labeled *Customary→Metric.* Review the different units of measure for each category. Ask: *What are some customary and metric units of measure for length? Weight? Capacity?*

4. Demonstrate how to complete each chart. For example, say: *Look at the first conversion card, 1 foot (ft) = 12 inches. In which chart does it belong?* (Length) *In which box?* (Customary) Place the card in the correct box of the *Length* chart.

5. Then have students cut apart their cards and glue them in the appropriate charts. Suggest that they sort all of the cards before gluing any of them.

6. Have students check their answers with a partner before reviewing the answers together as a class. Then demonstrate how to use the completed charts to solve math problems, such as *6 1/4 lb = ___ oz, 4 1/2 miles = ___ km,* and *4 qt = ___ L.*

7. Ask students to write and solve other conversion problems. You might also have them write story problems about converting units of measure. For example, they could write about converting units of measure during a trip to Europe. They could write two sets of directions for the same toy model, one written in customary units of measure and the other written in metric units of measure.

Extended Learning

Have students draw or cut out pictures of items representing different types of measurement. For example, for capacity, items might include a water bottle, a soda can, and a glass of milk. Have them also draw items that represent about one unit of each measure. For example: the width of one finger ≈ one centimeter; the width of two fingers ≈ one inch; the length of one shoe ≈ one foot; the weight of a pair of shoes ≈ one pound; the weight of a paper clip ≈ one gram; the weight of a kitten ≈ one kilogram.

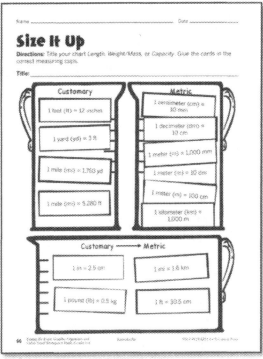

Size It Up

Directions: Title your chart *Length*, *Weight/Mass*, or *Capacity*. Glue the cards in the correct measuring cups.

Title: _____

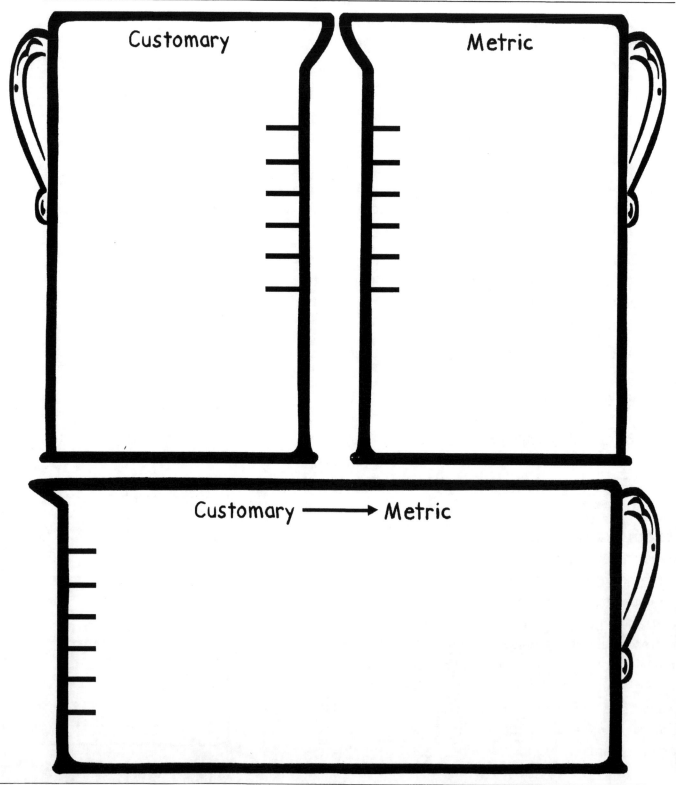

Conversion Cards

Directions: Use these cards to complete your Size It Up charts.

1 foot (ft) = 12 inches	1 pound (lb) = 16 oz	1 mi = 1.6 km
1 gram (g) = 10 dg	1 yard (yd) = 3 ft	1 decimeter (dm) = 10 cm
1 meter (m) = 1,000 mm	1 pound (lb) = 0.5 kg	1 gram (g) = 100 cg
1 kilogram (kg) = 1,000 g	1 in = 2.5 cm	1 mile (mi) = 1,760 yd
1 tablespoon (tbsp) = 3 tsp	1 meter (m) = 100 cm	1 cup (c) = 16 tbsp
1 ounce (oz) = 28.4 g	1 quart (qt) = 2 pt	1 kilometer (km) = 1,000 m
1 quart (qt) = 0.9 L	1 mile (mi) = 5,280 ft	1 yd = 0.9 m
1 gram (g) = 1,000 mg	1 liter (L) = 1,000 mL	1 ton (t) = 2,000 lb
1 pint (pt) = 2 c	1 ft = 30.5 cm	1 meter (m) = 10 dm
1 kiloliter (kL) = 1,000 L	1 centimeter (cm) = 10 mm	1 gallon (gal) = 4 qt

Metric Math: Step Chart

Materials

Metric Step Chart
reproducible

Skills Objectives

Use number patterns to describe and compare metric units.
Write metric units using exponents and powers of ten.

A **Step Chart** can help students progress from one unit to another as they calculate and compare different metric units of measure. The sequential steps visually show the relationship between each unit value and the common base.

1. Write *What is a meter?* on the board, and explain that a meter is part of the metric system of length. Have students extend their arms outward from each side, and explain that the distance across their arms is about one meter.

2. Give students a copy of the **Metric Step Chart reproducible (page 70)**, and display a copy to guide instruction. Explain that the metric system is based on multiples or *powers* of 10, either increasing or decreasing tenfold from one unit to the next.

3. Work with students to complete the Metric Step Chart reproducible, writing the transitions from one metric unit to the next. Write the prefix on the top of each step and the corresponding values inside the step. Explain that the "base" step stands for one meter (m), one gram (g), or one liter (L), depending on the category being measured—it's the base word of that category (e.g., kilo**meter**).

   Kilo—1000, 10^3
   Hecto—100, 10^2
   Deca—10, 10^1
   (base)— 1, 10^0
   Deci—1/10, 10^{-1}
   Centi—1/100, 10^{-2}
   Milli—1/1000, 10^{-3}

4. Tell students that as they go up the steps, the values increase "x 10"; as they go down, the values decrease "÷ 10." You might

also have them write the decimal values for the steps below the base (*deci, 0.1; centi, 0.01; milli, 0.001*).

5. Use the chart to review metric conversions. For example, to get from *centi* to the base is two steps upward, which is 10 x 10 = 100, so 100 centimeters = 1 meter. Comparatively, if you start at the base and go upward two steps to *hecto*, it's 10 x 10 = 100 meters, so 100 meters = 1 hectometer.

6. Invite students to use their completed chart to help them solve story problems such as these: *The Eiffel Tower in Paris, France, is about 300 meters tall. How many centimeters tall is the Eiffel Tower?* (1 m = 100 cm, so 300 m = 100 x 300 = 30,000 cm.) *If a metal beam is about 500 centimeters long, how many beams would it take to reach the top of the Eiffel Tower if the beams were stacked end to end?* (Since 100 cm = 1 m, then 500 cm = 5 m, so 300 m ÷ 5 m = 60 beams.) Have students work in pairs or small groups to solve the story problems.

7. Invite volunteers to share their solutions and explain how they solved the problems. You might also have students write their own problems for classmates to solve.

Extended Learning

Have students work in small groups to build a toothpick model of the Eiffel Tower or another high-rise building. Have them use a conversion scale such as *1 cm:1 m* (model:actual size). Tell them that each toothpick is about 5 cm long. After they complete their model, have students write and solve measurement problems comparing the dimensions of their model to the actual size. You might also have them gather more facts and figures about the Eiffel Tower at Web sites such as *www.tour-eiffel.com.*

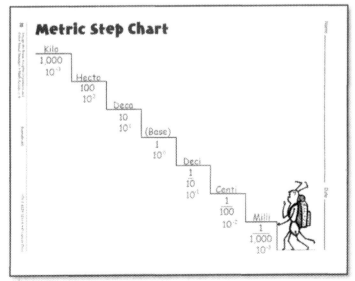

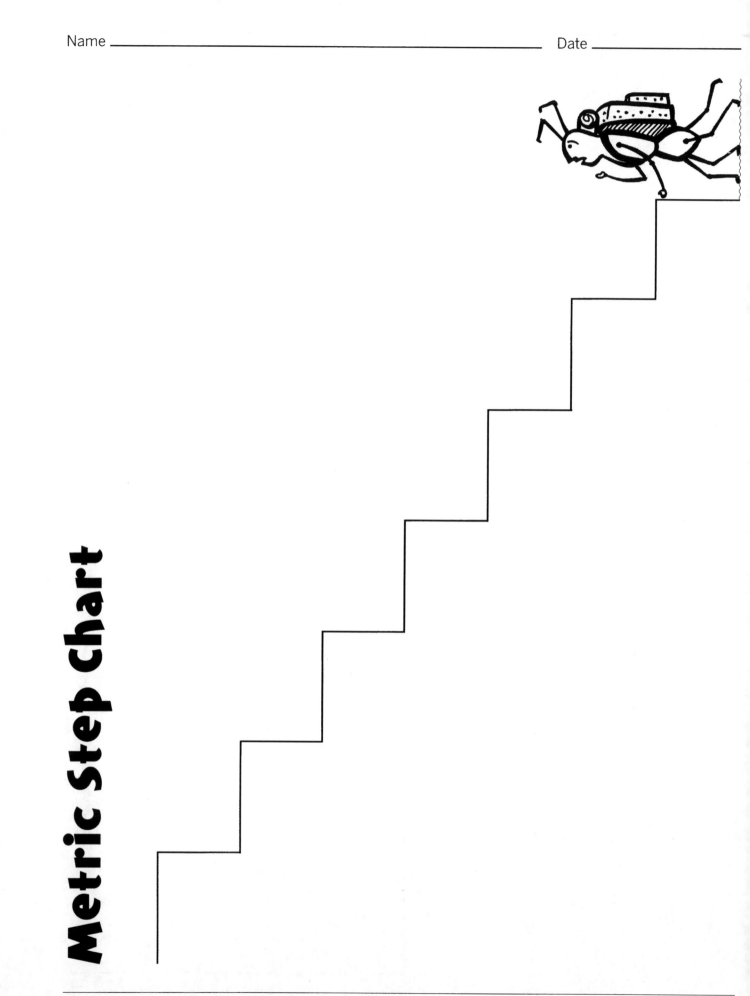

Metric Step Chart

Spatial Math: Grid Squares

Skills Objectives
Estimate, measure, and compare the perimeter and area of regular and irregular shapes.
Use mathematical models and spatial reasoning to measure and draw shapes.

Materials
Math Art reproducible

math journals

jigsaw puzzle pieces

centimeter grid paper

string

scissors

metric rulers

colored pencils

Using **Grid Squares** can help students estimate, calculate, and compare the perimeter and area of irregular shapes. In this activity, students use grid squares to find the perimeter and area of block letters and create their own math art.

1. Ask students: *What is the difference between the area and perimeter of a polygon?* Explain that the *area* is the surface covered by the inside of the shape (like a grassy lawn); the *perimeter* is the distance around the shape (like a fence around the lawn). Have students record in their journals the following formulas for the area of regular polygons: *(b = base, h= height, r = radius); parallelogram, A = bh; triangle, A = 1/2bh; trapezoid, 1/2h(b$_1$ + b$_2$); circle, A = 3.14r^2.* Demonstrate how to use the formulas. For example: *What is the area of half a 10 cm x 5 cm rectangle divided by its diagonal?* (A triangle with an area of 25 cm^2)

2. Explain to students that sometimes they need to estimate the perimeter and area of an irregular shape. Using grid squares can help them make more reasonable estimates. Give each student a jigsaw puzzle piece and a sheet of centimeter grid paper. Instruct them to carefully trace their puzzle piece on the grid paper and use the grid squares to estimate the perimeter and area. Point out that each grid square is one centimeter long. Tell them to write their answers on the back of their paper.

3. Have pairs of students exchange papers and check each other's estimations. If they disagree, have them work together to figure out the most reasonable estimate. Invite partners to explain to the class how they decided on their answers.

4. Ask students: *How can you use string and a ruler to check your estimates?* Demonstrate how to use string to outline the shape, cut and measure that length of string with a ruler to find the perimeter, and then use it to form a regular polygon (such as a

rectangle) to measure the sides and calculate the area using a formula.

5. Give students string and a metric ruler to measure their shapes and compare their answers with their estimates. Invite volunteers to share their results.

6. Next, distribute copies of the **Math Art reproducible (page 73)**, and tell students to estimate and calculate the perimeter and area of the whole word, using the grid squares to estimate and using string to help them measure. Suggest that they divide the letters into regular shapes to help them estimate more accurately.

7. Invite students to share and compare their results. Ask them to explain how they estimated, measured, and calculated the perimeter and area of the word.

8. Then have students draw their own irregular-shaped figure or word on grid paper and then give their paper to a classmate to find the perimeter and area. Have students exchange papers to check each other's work. Frame and display the finished artwork.

Extended Learning

• Have the class brainstorm real-world situations in which the area of an irregular shape, such as a lake or pond, needs to be determined. You might also have them research and compare the perimeter and area of different U.S. states.

• Have students draw rectangles of increasing size to discover a pattern of increase for perimeter and area. (The perimeter increases by two; the area increases by a multiple of four.) Have them make a data table to list and share their results.

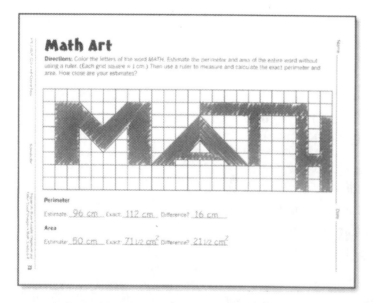

Name _____   Date _____

Math Art

Directions: Color the letters of the word *MATH*. Estimate the perimeter and area of the entire word without using a ruler. (Each grid square = 1 cm.) Then use a ruler to measure and calculate the exact perimeter and area. How close are your estimates?

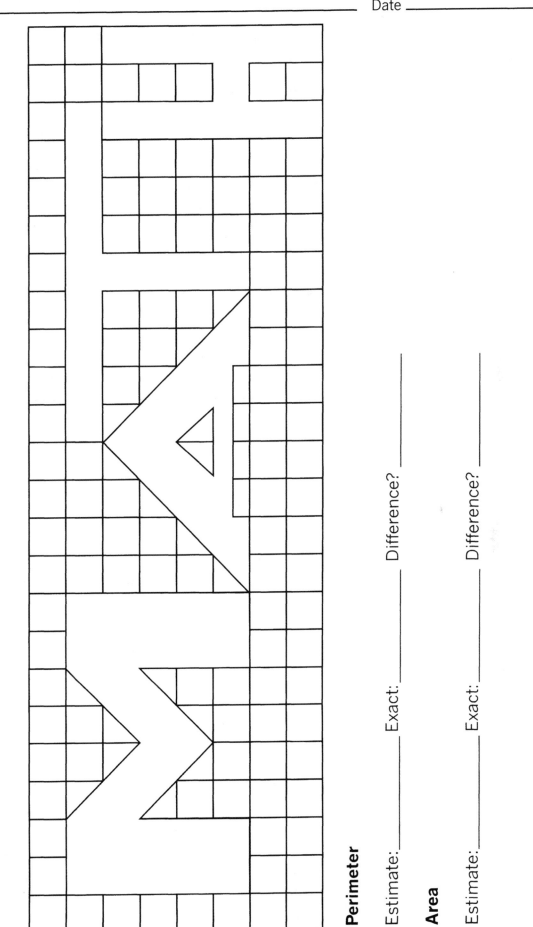

Perimeter

Estimate: _____   Exact: _____   Difference? _____

Area

Estimate: _____   Exact: _____   Difference? _____

Gift Boxes: 3-D Models

Materials

Nets of Solid Figures reproducibles

metric rulers

scissors

tape

math journals

calculators

gift boxes and gift wrap (optional)

Skills Objectives

Measure and calculate the surface area and volume of solid figures. Use nets to make three-dimensional models of solid figures.

Creating and using a **Three-Dimensional (3-D) Model** offers students the opportunity to examine and explore geometric figures from different perspectives. This gives them a greater understanding of surface area and volume dimensions. It also helps students relate the model to real-life objects and problems related to everyday life. In this activity, students use models to help them visualize and calculate the surface area and volume of gift boxes and other 3-D containers.

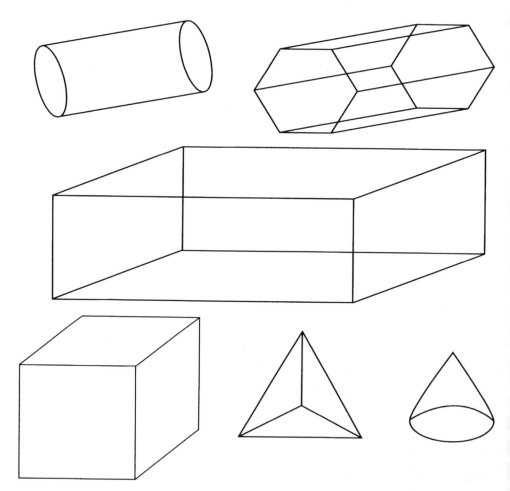

1. Ask students: *What are the shapes of gift boxes you have used or received?* (Possible answers: *rectangular prisms, cubes*) *How can you determine the amount of wrapping paper needed to cover the box without actually putting the box on the paper?* Explain that by figuring out the surface area—the area of all the faces of the box added together—they can determine how much paper is needed.

2. Give students a copy of both **Nets of Solid Figures reproducibles (pages 77–78)**. Explain that a *net* is a flattened version of a three-dimensional figure that can be folded to make that figure. The net shows each surface, or *face*, of the figure. Ask volunteers to tell the name of each solid figure formed from the nets. (cube, triangular prism, cylinder, rectangular prism, cone, hexagonal prism)

3. Before students fold their nets into solid figures, have them use a metric ruler and formulas for area to find the total surface area of each net. (To find the area of a regular hexagon, have students use the formula $A \approx 2.598 \times s^2$, where s is the length of one side.) Show students how to set up and complete a table of formulas and measurements in their math journal for each net. For example:

Triangular Prism

Face	Shape of Face	Formula	Area of the Face
1	triangle	$A = 1/2bh$	
2			
3			
4			
5			

4. Have students work in pairs or small groups to check and compare their results. Point out that their answers may be slightly different, depending on the accuracy of their measurements.

5. Have students assemble their nets into solid figures. Demonstrate how to fold along the dashed lines and tape the edges together. Use the assembled models to review the parts of each solid figure—the number of faces, edges, and vertices.

6. Ask students: *How much do you think will fit inside each of these figures?* Explain that they can use their measurements and specific formulas for volume to figure out how much each figure can hold.

7. Write the following formulas on the board for students to copy into their math journals: *Cylinder* $V = \pi r^2 h$; *Cone* $V = 1/3(\pi r^2 h)$; *Cube* $V = s^3$; *Volume of Any Prism* $V = Bh$, where B is the area of the base and h is the height of the prism. Have them use the

formulas and the dimensions of their models to find the volume of each figure.

8. Suggest that students use their models to help them solve story problems such as the following. You might also have them use actual gift boxes and wrapping paper to create and solve problems. Review and discuss the solutions together.

- *What is the minimum amount of wrapping paper needed to cover a toy house that is ten times the size of the triangular prism stacked on top of the cube?*
- *What is the minimum amount of wrapping paper needed to cover a toy rocket that is ten times the size of the cone stacked on top of the cylinder?*
- *What is the minimum amount of paper needed to cover a cubic jack-in-the-box stacked on top of a rectangular board game, both ten times the size of the models?*

Extended Learning

Have students calculate the area of a regular hexagon as follows:

- Divide the hexagon into six equilateral triangles from the center to each vertex.

- Measure the length of the base and the height of one triangle.

- Calculate the area of that triangle.

- Multiply the area by six to get the area of the hexagon.

- Have students compare their answer to the answer for $A = 2.598 \times s^2$, and discuss any possible differences.

Nets of Solid Figures

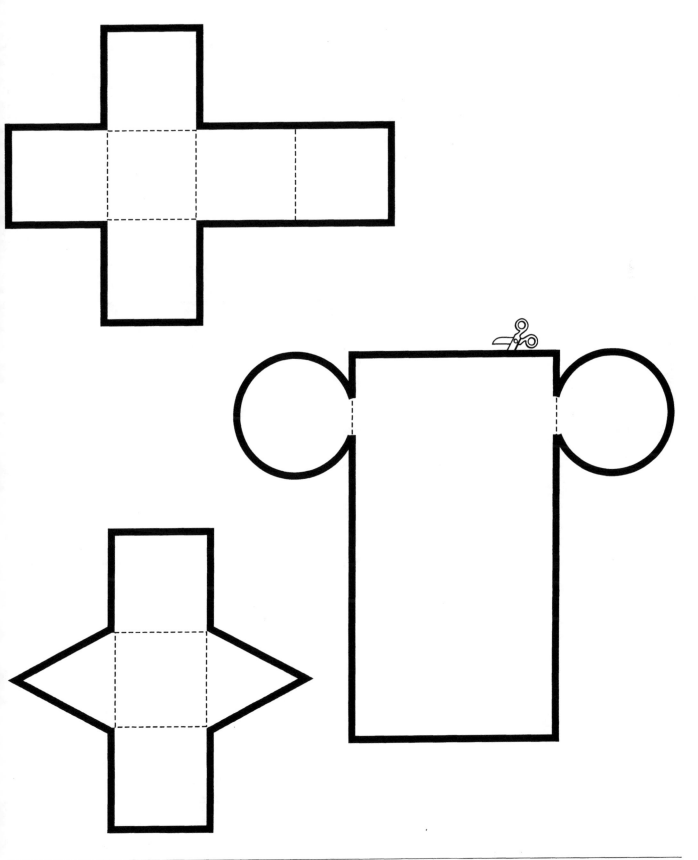

Nets of Solid Figures

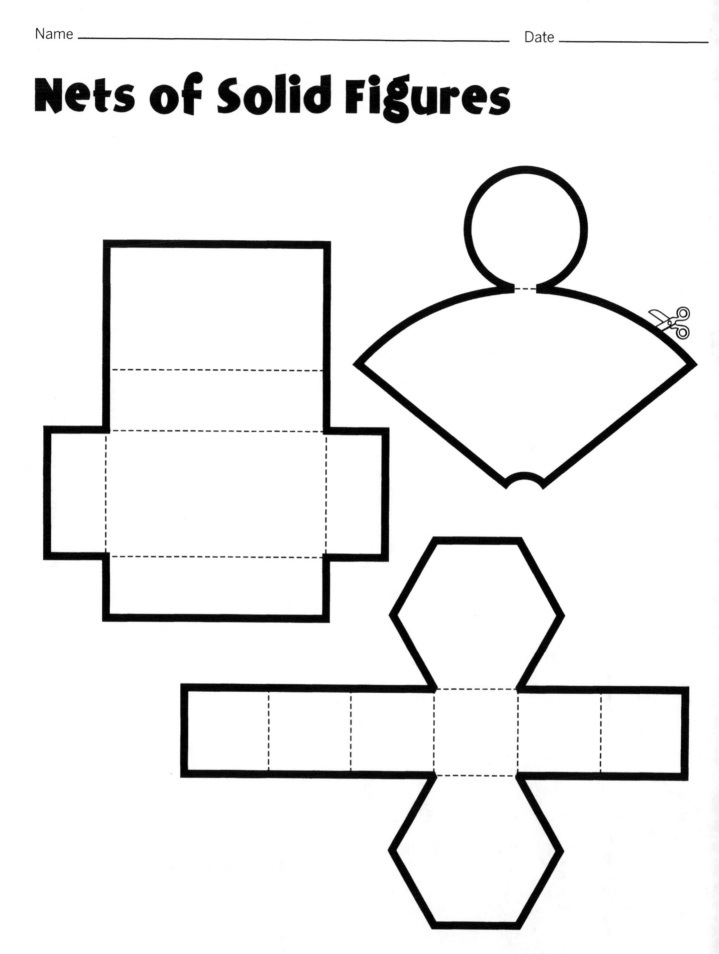

 Engage the Brain: Graphic Organizers and Other Visual Strategies • Math, Grades 6–8   Reproducible   978-1-4129-5231-6 • © Corwin Press

CHAPTER 5

Data Analysis and Probability

Fitness Challenge: Stem-and-Leaf Plot

Skills Objectives
Construct, read, and interpret single and double stem-and-leaf plots. Find the range, median, and mode for a set of data.

A **Stem-and-Leaf Plot** lists numerical data in a graphic display based on quantities of tens and ones (expanded form). The "stems" are the tens digits, and the "leaves" are the ones digits arranged in numerical order. In this activity, students create a double stem-and-leaf plot to compare the results of two fitness activities.

Materials
Fitness Stem-and-Leaf Plot reproducible
sticky notes
colored pencils

1. Tell students that a *stem-and-leaf plot* is similar to those parts of a plant—the stem is the main part of the number, represented by the tens digits, and the leaves are the extensions or the ones digits.

2. Use the following data to show how to make a simple stem-and-leaf plot, writing the tens digits as the stems and the ones digits as the leaves. Invite students to help write the leaves for each stem in order, from smallest to largest. Point out that the completed plot visually shows the distribution of the data.

Number of Sit-Ups per Minute for Mrs. Wilson's Class
13, 27, 30, 44, 40, 39, 26, 12, 10, 24, 8, 34, 45, 44, 32, 29, 20, 39, 44, 38, 34, 47, 40

Stem	Leaf
0	8
1	0, 2, 3
2	0, 4, 6, 7, 9
3	0, 2, 4, 4, 8, 9, 9
4	0, 0, 4, 4, 4, 5, 7

Key: 2 | 4 = 24

3. Demonstrate how to use the completed stem-and-leaf plot to analyze the data, finding the *range* (difference between the highest and lowest value), *median* (middle value), and *mode* (value occurring most often).

4. Tell students that they are going to create a double stem-and-leaf plot showing the results of two fitness activities. They will write one set of data on the right side of the stems and the other set of data on the left side of the stems. For an example, write some values on the left side of the stem-and-leaf plot on the board.

5. Give students a copy of the **Fitness Stem-and-Leaf Plot reproducible (page 81)**. Decide what two activities to test for one minute, such as sit-ups, push-ups, jumping jacks, rope jumps, or side steps. Have students write the names of the activities above the stem-and-leaf plot, one name on each side.

6. Time students for one minute as they complete each activity, and have partners write the results on sticky notes for you to post on the board or chart paper to show both sets of data. (Students do not need to write their names.)

7. Have students use the results to complete their double stem-and-leaf plot. Monitor their progress, and offer guidance as needed. Encourage them to draw leaves around their numbers to create a more artistic version of the results.

8. Have students find the range, median, and mode for each data set. Then have them compare the results and write a summary of their findings. Discuss the results as a class.

Extended Learning

Have students create their own double stem-and-leaf plot for a pair of surveys at school or for a fitness challenge between your class and another class. Have them use construction paper to create an artistic "tree display" of the results.

Name _____ Date _____

Fitness Stem-and-Leaf Plot

Directions: Make a double stem-and-leaf plot to show the results of two fitness tests, one set of data on each side. Draw leaves around the numbers on each branch to show the values.

Activity: _____ **Activity:** _____

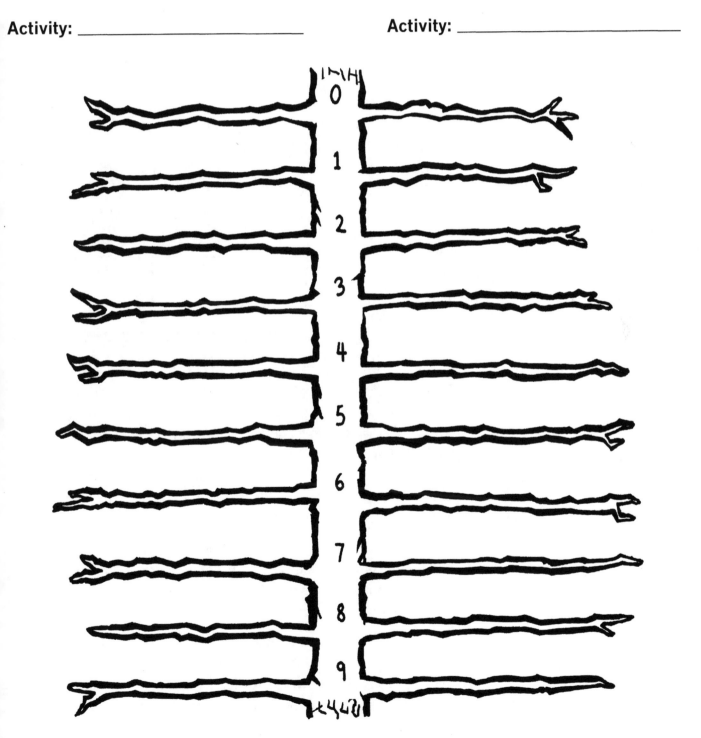

0
1
2
3
4
5
6
7
8
9

Raccoon Math: Box-and-Whisker Plot

Skills Objectives

Create and analyze a box-and-whisker plot for a given set of values. Use mathematical models to represent and interpret quantitative relationships.

Materials

Raccoon Math reproducibles

Box-and-Whisker Plot reproducible

rulers

calculators (optional)

A **Box-and-Whisker Plot** displays data in four sections or quartiles along a number line, providing a visual picture of the central tendency and the distribution of data around it. For this activity, students create a box-and-whisker plot about a group of raccoons. They display and analyze the distribution of raccoons in their plot.

1. Review the meanings of *central tendency* and *median* with students. Write the following data on the board, and demonstrate how to find the median: *12, 17, 9, 8, 10, 9, 7, 5, 15, 16, 6, 18, 20, 25.* Remind students that the data must be written in sequential order, from least to greatest, to find the median (middle value); if there is an even number of values, the median is the average of the two middle values.

   (*5, 6, 7, 8, 9, 9, 10, 12, 15, 16, 17, 18, 20, 25; median = 11*)

2. Explain to students that they can analyze the data more completely by creating a box-and-whisker plot. Give students a copy of the **Raccoon Math** and **Box-and-Whisker Plot reproducibles (pages 84–86)**, and display copies to guide instruction. Point out that the values on the board are the same values as those shown in the table of raccoon weights. Have students list those weights in a row from least to greatest for Problem 1.

3. Then have students write the minimum value (5), the Median (11), and the maximum value (25) for Problem 2. Point out that the difference between the highest value (maximum) and the lowest value (minimum) is called the *range*.

4. Draw a line through the middle of the row of values at the median location, dividing the data set into two parts of 50%. Tell students that they can further divide the data by finding the middle (median) of both the upper and lower halves. The middle value

of the lower 50% (between the median and the minimum value) is called the *lower quartile*; the middle value of the upper 50% (between the median and the maximum value) is called the *upper quartile*.

5. Have students find the lower and upper quartiles for Problem 3. *(LQ = 8; UQ = 17)* Point out that the lower quartile, the median, and the upper quartile divide the data into four parts of 25%.

6. Work with students to complete the Box-and-Whisker Plot reproducible using the minimum, lower quartile, median, upper quartile, and maximum values, as described at the bottom of Raccoon Math 1. Demonstrate how to plot the five points and use a ruler to connect them about an inch above the number line. Invite students to help decide what numbers to use for the number line (equal increments) and draw and connect the points to display the completed plot.

7. After they complete their plots, have students work independently or with a partner to complete the Raccoon Math 2 reproducible. Then review and discuss the answers together as a class.

Extended Learning

- Ask students to create a box-and-whisker plot to analyze a given set of lengths for raccoons (or another animal), given a range of values from 20 to 40 inches. Then have them write and answer questions about their plot.

- Invite students to make a raccoon face out of their box-and-whisker plot, similar to the art shown ont he previous page.

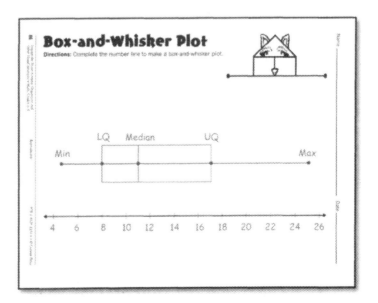

Raccoon Math 1

Directions: Use the raccoon data to solve the problems below.

Raccoon	Weight (lbs)
Kramer	12
Bandit	17
Ginger	9
Rascal	8
Ebony	10
Midnight	9
Junior	7
Salinger	5
Thor	15
Scout	16
Topaz	6
Jonah	18
Sophie	20
Garfield	25

1. List the weights of the raccoons in a row from least to greatest.

2. Write the *minimum value*, the *median*, and the *maximum value* for the data.

   Minimum: _____   Median: _____   Maximum: _____

3. Find the *lower quartile* (middle value between the *minimum* and the *median*) and the *upper quartile* (middle value between the *median* and the *maximum*).

   Lower Quartile: _____   Upper Quartile: _____

4. Use a number line and a ruler to make a box-and-whisker plot of the *minimum*, *lower quartile*, *median*, *upper quartile*, and *maximum* values:

   Step 1: Above the number line, draw dots for the five values in a row.

   Step 2: Draw parallel, 1-cm vertical marks through each *lower quartile*, the *median*, and the *upper quartile*. Connect the ends to make a two-part box.

   Step 3: Make a "whisker" on each end of the box by drawing a line segment from the *lower quartile* to the *minimum* and from the *upper quartile* to the *maximum*.

 Engage the Brain: Graphic Organizers and Other Visual Strategies • Math, Grades 6–8   Reproducible   978-1-4129-5231-6 • © Corwin Press

Raccoon Math 2

Directions: Analyze the data from Raccoon Math 1.

1. Which data values are in each section of the plot (between the points)?

   Lower Whisker   Part 1 of the Box   Part 2 of the Box   Upper Whisker

   _____   _____   _____   _____

2. About what percent of the data is in each section of the plot? _____

3. Why are the whiskers different lengths?

   _____

   _____

   _____

4. What is the range of weight for the entire group of raccoons? Median weight?

   _____

5. What is the range of weight for the top 50%? Median weight?

   _____

6. What percent of the raccoons weigh less than 8 pounds? More than 17 pounds?

   _____

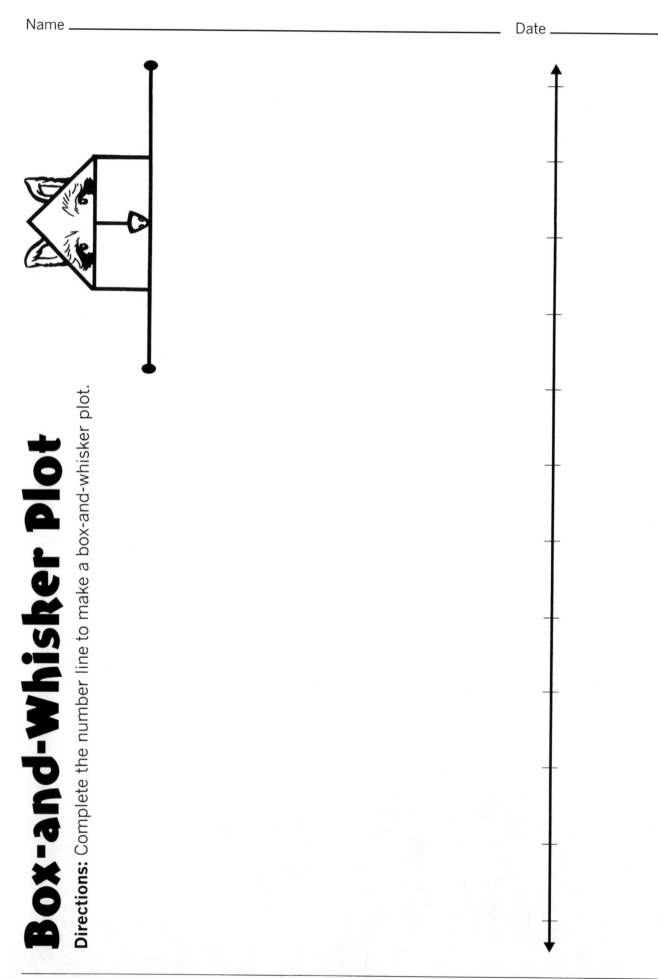

Box-and-Whisker Plot

Directions: Complete the number line to make a box-and-whisker plot.

Spin It! Outcome Grids

Skills Objectives
Distinguish between theoretical and experimental probability.
Use outcome grids and tree diagrams to determine the probability of each possible outcome of two or more combined events.

Materials
Spin It! reproducible

math journals

small paper clips

An **Outcome Grid** is an organizational chart for listing and analyzing theoretical probabilities, showing all possible outcomes of two independent events. For more than two events, a series of outcome grids may be used. In this activity, students use different spinners to explore both theoretical and experimental probabilities.

1. Write *probability, theoretical probability,* and *experimental probability* on the board, and discuss the meaning of each term with students. (Refer to the words *probable* and *probably* to help students understand the meaning of *probability*—the likelihood of an event happening.) Explain that *theoretical probability* is the expected or predicted outcome, whereas *experimental probability* is the tested or actual outcome. Then tell students that they will use spinners to explore both theoretical and experimental probability.

2. Give students a small paper clip and a copy of the **Spin It! reproducible (page 90)**. Display a copy to guide instruction. Refer students to the three spinners at the top of the page, noting the equal sections of thirds, fourths, and fifths. Explain that any category of choices may be written in the blank sections of each spinner.

3. Use the first spinner to demonstrate how to complete and use an outcome grid. Write *1, 2,* and *3* in the sections of the first spinner (one number per section). Ask: *If we spin this spinner twice, what are the possible results of those two numbers added together?* (You may also use products or ordered pairs.) Explain to students that they can use an outcome grid to list the possible outcomes.

4. Show students how to write the three possible numbers for the first spin along the top of the first grid (*1, 2, 3*) and the three possible numbers for the second spin down the left side of the grid (in this case, the same three numbers). Note that there will be blank boxes left over. Explain that if you were using two different spinners instead of the same spinner twice, you would list the numbers for the second spinner down the left side of the grid.

5. Have students fill in the 3-by-3 grid of sums for each pair of numbers. Ask: *How many total outcomes are possible?* (9) *What are they?* (2, 3, 3, 4, 4, 4, 5, 5, 6)

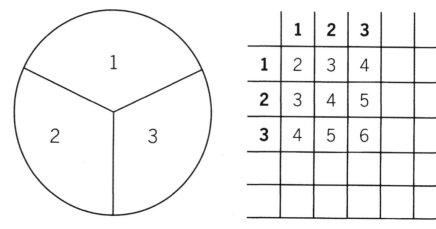

	1	2	3		
1	2	3	4		
2	3	4	5		
3	4	5	6		

6. Ask: *What is the probability of getting each possible sum?* Demonstrate how to compare the total number for each sum with the total number of all possible sums to determine each probability. As you list the probabilities, have students copy them in their math journals under the title *Theoretical Probability: Sum 2 = 1/9; Sum 3 = 2/9; Sum 4 = 3/9; Sum 5 = 2/9; Sum 6 = 1/9.*

7. Have students use the spinner to find the *experimental probabilities*, recording sums for nine pairs of spins. (Demonstrate how to spin the spinner using a paper clip and pencil.)

8. Suggest that students create a tally chart to mark each sum they spin. Have them determine each experimental probability by comparing the number of spins per sum versus the total number of possible sums.

9. Discuss the results as a class, comparing students' experimental probabilities to the theoretical probabilities. Ask students to explain why they might be different.

10. Ask students to use their spinners and outcome grids to create a probability activity involving numbers, letters, colors, or other choices for their spinners. Invite volunteers to share their results.

Extended Learning

Show students how to use more than one outcome grid or a tree diagram to determine the possible outcomes of three or more independent events. Use this story problem to guide instruction, relating it to the double-spin activity:

> Cheryl is a contestant on Spin to Win! She is given a spinner divided into three equal sections of red, green, and blue. She is asked to spin it three times. To win, she must spin the same color

all three times. What are her chances? (3 out of 27, or 1:9)

- **Option 1:** Have students use two outcome grids sequentially, using the first one to show the outcomes of two spins and then using those results in combination with a third spin to show the final 27 outcomes on the second outcome grid.

	R	G	B
R	RR	RG	RB
G	GR	GG	GB
B	BR	BG	BB

	RR	RG	RB	GR	GG	GB	BR	BG	BB
R	RRR	RRG	RRB	RGR	RGG	RGB	RBR	RBG	RBB
G	GRR	GRG	GRB	GGR	GGG	GGB	GBR	GBG	GBB
B	BRR	BRG	BRB	BGR	BGG	BGB	BBR	BBG	BBB

- **Option 2:** Have students complete a tree diagram, like that shown below, to determine all 27 possible outcomes, listing the combination along each branch.

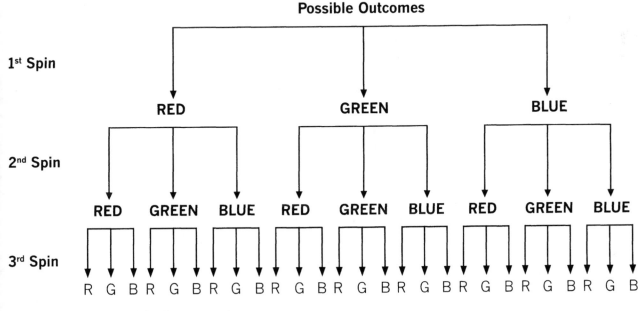

Possible Outcomes

Tree Results (Possible Outcomes)
Left section: RRR   RRG   RRB   RGR   RGG   RGB   RBR   RBG   RBB
Mid section: GRR   GRG   GRB   GGR   GGG   GGB   GBR   GBG   GBB
Right section: BRR   BRG   BRB   BGR   BGG   BGB   BBR   BBG   BBB

Spin It!

Outcome Grids

Mystery Hotel: Probability Map

Skills Objectives
Solve problems involving theoretical probability.
Use a model to find the area of regular and irregular shapes.
Determine the probability of an event by comparing relative areas.

Materials

Mystery Hotel reproducible

My Mystery Hotel reproducible

color tiles (optional)

colored pencils

rulers

In this activity, students use a **Probability Map** to determine the theoretical probability of finding a hidden object within a given amount of space. They find the relative area of each room in a hotel in order to determine the probability or likelihood of finding an object hidden in one of the rooms.

1. Review an example of simple probability by drawing a square divided into four equal sections and coloring three of them. Ask students: *If you throw a penny on this box, what is the probability of getting a colored square?* (3/4) *An uncolored square?* (1/4) Tell students that they will be expanding on this concept by creating and using a probability map.

   8/30

   22/30

2. Give students a copy of the **Mystery Hotel reproducible (page 93)**, and display a copy to guide instruction. Explain that the map at the top of the page is a floor plan of a hotel. There is an object hidden somewhere underneath one of the floor tiles. Point out that each grid square represents one floor tile. Tell student they will calculate the probability of finding the hidden object in each room.

3. Ask students: *How can we figure out the probability of finding the object in each room?* Guide students through the process of counting all the floor tiles (grid squares) in each room (the *area*) and comparing that amount to the total number of tiles throughout all the rooms. You might also have students use color tiles to model the floor plan, using a different color for each room.

4. Ask students: *How many floor tiles are in Mr. Einstein's room?* (5 x 4 = 20 tiles) *How many floor tiles are in all the rooms all together?* (10 x 10 = 100 tiles) *What is the probability of finding the hidden object in Mr. Einstein's room?* (20/100, or 1:5) Have students record the answer in Mr. Einstein's room. Repeat the process for the other rooms.

5. Invite students to work independently or in pairs to answer the

probability questions. For Problem 6, point out the word *adjacent* to students, and suggest that they use their map or color tiles to help them solve the problem.

6. Review answers together as a class, and invite volunteers to share their solutions. Make sure students understand that the answers for Problems 3 and 4 involve adding the fractional probabilities together for all rooms.

7. Invite students to create their own probability map and mystery questions on the **My Mystery Hotel reproducible (page 94)**. Make sure they understand that they must use the entire 10 x 10 grid for their map. Suggest that they create a model with color tiles to help them decide on a layout. You might also encourage them to include more than one hidden object and to ask questions involving *dependent events*, in which the probability of one answer depends on the probability of another, such as the number of available tiles decreasing with each hidden object.

8. Invite students to exchange papers and solve each other's mysteries. Display their completed work as part of an interactive bulletin board.

Extend Learning

Invite students to write a mystery story that involves probability. Encourage them to include a probability map. Bind their stories together to make a class book.

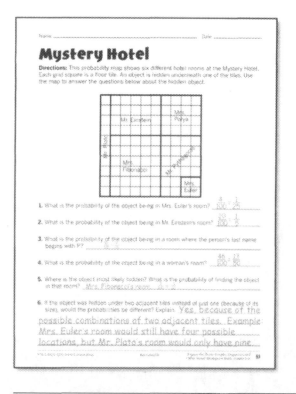

Mystery Hotel

Directions: This probability map shows six different hotel rooms at the Mystery Hotel. Each grid square is a floor tile. An object is hidden underneath one of the tiles. Use the map to answer the questions below about the hidden object.

1. What is the probability of the object being in Mrs. Euler's room? _____

2. What is the probability of the object being in Mr. Einstein's room? _____

3. What is the probability of the object being in the room of a person whose last name begins with P? _____

4. What is the probability of the object being in a woman's room? _____

5. Where is the object most likely hidden? What is the probability of finding the object in that room? _____

6. If the object was hidden under two adjacent tiles instead of just one (because of its size), would the probabilities be different? Explain. _____

_____

_____

_____

My Mystery Hotel

Directions: Make a probability map for your own mystery. Then write probability questions about it. Write the answers on the back of this paper.

1. _____

_____

2. _____

_____

3. _____

_____

4. _____

_____

5. _____

_____

Answer Key

Running Project Analysis (page 13)

1. Keisha = 12 laps or 3 miles per day; Adam = 16 laps or 4 miles per day; Bob = 10 laps or 2.5 miles per day.
2. After six days, Keisha should have completed 72 laps, Adam 96 laps, and Bob 60 laps. Keisha is passing her goal (84 laps > 72 laps). Adam and Bob are behind their goals (80 laps < 96 laps; 40 laps < 60 laps).
3. Keisha has completed the most; Bob has completed the least.

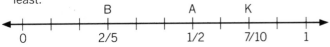

4. Keisha 120 – 84 = 36 laps left; Adam 160 – 80 = 80 laps left; Bob 100 – 40 = 60 laps left
5. Keisha 180 laps, 180/120; Adam 240 laps, 240/160; Bob 150 laps, 150/100
   All fractions are greater than 1.

Input–Output Problems (page 30)

1. $f(x) = 2x^2 - 1$; Input: –2, –1, 0, 1, 2; Output: 7, 1, –1, 1, 7
2. $f(x) = 3x + 2$; Input: –2, –1, 0, 1, 2; Output: –4, 1, 2, 5, 8
3. $f(x) = 2x + 2$; Input: –2, –1, 0, 1, 2; Output: –2, 0, 2, 4, 6
4. $f(x) = 5x - 2$; Input: –2, –1, 0, 1, 2; Output: –12, –7, –2, 3, 8
5. $c = \$10p + \$4$, where c = cost and p = packages; so $f(x) = 10x + 4$
   2 packages = $24; 4 packages = $44; 5 packages = $54
6. $c = \$1.50r + 40$, where c = cost and r = ring tones; so $f(x) = 1.5x + 40$
   3 ring tones = $44.50; 7 ring tones = $50.50; 9 ring tones = $53.50
7. $c = \$60m + \$100$, where c = cost and m = months; so $f(x) = 60x + 100$
   3 months = $280; 7 months = $520; 12 months = $820
8. Answers will vary.

Diagonal Division (page 55)

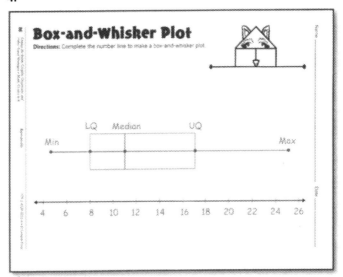

Diagonal Division Table

Directions: Use the polygon shapes to help you complete this table. For each polygon, draw all the diagonals from a single vertex. Count the number of triangles formed. Then calculate the total degrees of all the angles in the polygon. Use your results to figure out the formula for the total degrees of an n-gon.

Polygon	Number of Sides of the Polygon	Number of Triangles Formed	Total Degrees of All Angles in the Polygon
Triangle	3	1	1 triangle × (180°) = 180°
Quadrilateral	4	2	2 × 180° = 360°
Pentagon	5	3	3 × 180° = 540°
Hexagon	6	4	4 × 180° = 720°
Heptagon	7	5	5 × 180° = 900°
Octagon	8	6	6 × 180° = 1,080°
n-gon	n	n–2	(n–2) × 180°

If all the polygons are regular polygons, what is the measure of each angle in the polygon?

Triangle __60__   Pentagon __108__   Heptagon __128.6__
Quadrilateral __90__   Hexagon __120__   Octagon __135__

Spatial Math (page 71)

Perimeter of "MATH" = 112 cm (M = 36, A = 20, T = 28, H = 28)
Area of "MATH" = 71½ cm² (M = 32, A = 13½, T = 13, H = 13)
Estimates and differences will vary.

Raccoon Math 1 & 2 (pages 84–85)

1. From least to greatest: 5, 6, 7, 8, 9, 9, 10, 12, 15, 16, 17, 18, 20, 25
2. Minimum = 5; Median = (10 + 12) ÷ 2 = 11; Maximum = 25
3. Lower Quartile = 8; Upper Quartile = 17
4.

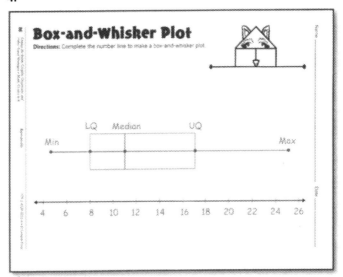

5. Lower Whisker = 5, 6, 7; Part 1 of the Box = 9, 9, 10; Part 2 of the Box = 12, 15, 16; Upper Whisker = 18, 20, 25
6. About 25% in each section.
7. The whisker at the lower end is shorter than the whisker at the upper end because the range between the lower quartile and the minimum value is less than the range between the upper quartile and the maximum value.
8. Range = 25 lbs – 5 lbs = 20 lbs; median = 11 lbs
9. Range of top 50% = 25 lbs – 11 lbs = 14 lbs; median (upper quartile) = 17 lbs
10. 25% weigh < 8 lbs (lower whisker); 25% weigh > 17 lbs (upper whisker)

Mystery Hotel (page 93)

1. Mrs. Euler's room = 4/100 or 1/25
2. Mr. Einstein's room = 20/100 or 1/5
3. Room with P name = 36/100 or 9/25
4. Woman's room = 46/100 or 13/50
5. Mrs. Fibonacci's room; 30/100 or 3/10
6. Yes, because of the different combinations of two adjacent tiles. For example, Mrs. Euler's room would still have four possible locations (four combinations of two tiles), whereas Mr. Plato's room would only have nine possible locations (not ten).

References

Bartels, B. (1995, November–December). Promoting mathematics connections with concept mapping. *Mathematics Teaching in the Middle School*, 542–549.

Beckman, P. (1971). *A history of pi*. Boulder, CO: The Golem Press.

Blatner, D. (1999). *The joy of π*. New York, NY: Walker & Company.

Bokhari, N. (2001). *Piece of pi: Wit-sharpening, brain bruising, number-crunching activities with pi*. San Luis Obispo, CA: Dandy Lion Publications.

Charles, R., & Lester, F. (1982). *Teaching problem solving: What, why, and how*. Palo Alto, CA: Dale Seymour Publications.

Gardner, H. (1983). *Frames of mind: The theory of multiple intelligences*. New York, NY: Basic Books.

Illinois State Board of Education. (n.d.). *Student assessment: Illinois assessment frameworks*. Retrieved January 4, 2007, from http://www.isbe.state.il.us.

Jacobson, J., & Raymer, D. (1999). *The big book of reproducible graphic organizers: 50 great templates to help kids get more out of reading, writing, social studies, and more*. New York, NY: Scholastic Professional Books.

Jensen, E., & Johnson, G. (1994). *The learning brain*. San Diego, CA: Turning Point for Teachers.

McCarthy, B. (1990). Using the 4MAT system to bring learning styles to schools. *Educational Leadership, 48*(2), 31–37.

National Council of Teachers of Mathematics. (2005). *Principles and standards for school mathematics*. Reston, VA: National Council of Teachers of Mathematics (NCTM).

Ogle, D. M. (2000). Make it visual: A picture is worth a thousand words. In M. McLaughlin & M. Vogt (Eds.), *Creativity and innovation in content area teaching*. Norwood, MA: Christopher-Gordon.

Parks, S, & Black, H. (1990). *Organizing thinking: Graphic organizers*. Pacific Grove, CA: Critical Thinking Press & Software.

Tate, M. L. (2003). *Worksheets don't grow dendrites: 20 instructional strategies that engage the brain*. Thousand Oaks, CA: Corwin Press.

Van de Walle, J. A. (1994). *Elementary school mathematics: Teaching developmentally*. White Plains, NY: Longman.

Printed in the United States
By Bookmasters